**Health and safety in school science and technology
for teachers of 3- to 12-year-olds**

Fourth edition

The **Association**
for **Science Education**

Members of the writing team for the 4th edition

Ann Barton-Greenwood — Retired lecturer in primary science, University of Wales Institute, Cardiff; Chair of Early Childhood Association, Cardiff & Vale of Glamorgan

Peter Borrows — Science education consultant; member and past-chair of ASE Safeguards in Science Committee (Project Leader)

Phil Bunyan — Director, CLEAPSS; member and past-chair of ASE Safeguards in Science Committee

Alison Christou — Senior Technician, Forest School, Snaresbrook, London; member of ASE Safeguards in Science Committee

Jenny Drayton — Science Coordinator, Riverside Community Primary School, Birstall, Leicestershire

Joe Jefferies — Science health and safety consultant; member of ASE Safeguards in Science Committee

John Lawrence — Deputy Chief Executive, ASE; member of ASE Safeguards in Science Committee

Liz Lawrence — Advisory Teacher for Science and Design and Technology (Primary), London Borough of Barking and Dagenham; Chair of ASE Primary Science Committee

Sinéad McGleenon — Teacher developer, Primary STEM Project, seconded from St Malachy's Primary School, Armagh

Hocine M'Zali — Senior Technician, Leeds City College; member of ASE Safeguards in Science Committee

Phil Stone — Science education consultant; member of ASE Safeguards in Science Committee

Ray Vincent — Teacher trainer, RSC, and science education consultant; secretary of ASE Safeguards in Science Committee

Ralph Whitcher — Health and Safety Manager, West Sussex County Council; chair of ASE Safeguards in Science Committee

Acknowledgements

This booklet is closely based on the third edition of *Be safe!*. The members of the writing teams for the third and earlier editions (unless listed above) were: Pauline Anderson, John Carleton, Allen Cochrane, Rona Davies, Christine Fogg, Tom Harrison, Kay Keith, Vicki Lewis, Michael Lexton, Dick Orton, Susan Plant, Mike Prince, John Richardson, Sheila Semple, Catherine Sinclair, Nick Stanley, John Tranter, John Wray and Barbara Wyvill. Barbara Shepherd (General Adviser for Home Economics in West Sussex) acted as consultant on matters of food hygiene for the second edition and the Scottish Science Advisers Group assisted with the Scottish edition. The editors were Hendrina Ellis (third edition), Carol Abbott (second edition) and John Richardson (Scottish edition).

We would like to thank CLEAPSS and SSERC, the Health and Safety Executive and various government education departments for their help with this and previous editions. Thanks are also due to the many people who sent ideas, commented on earlier editions or on drafts of this one or who told us about accidents and incidents in primary science. Special thanks to Anne Goldsworthy for permission to use the song on page 11. Irish, Canadian and Ontario editions were based on earlier editions of *Be safe!* and influenced this edition.

Most of the safety symbols used in this book are printed, with permission, using the CLEAPSS font, which is available to members.

We would welcome comments on this edition and reports of incidents or accidents resulting from practical activities in primary schools. Confidentiality will be respected – the sole purpose of collecting such information is to improve any future edition so that it better meets the needs of teachers.

Copy-editor and typesetter for this edition: Andrew Welsh

Original design and illustration: Sally Simpson

Additional illustrations: Paul Ellis, Deanna Melchior and Linda Page

Acknowledgement, page 4: Contains public sector information published by the Health and Safety Executive and licensed under the Open Government Licence v1.0

© The Association for Science Education, 2011

First edition, 1988

Second edition, 1990

Scottish edition, 1995

Third (UK) edition, 2001

Fourth (UK) edition, 2011

Reprinted 2011 twice,

Reprinted 2012

ISBN 978 0 86357 426 9

Printed by Ashford Colour Press, Gosport, Hampshire

This edition has been sponsored by CLEAPSS and SSERC.

Contents

This book gives guidance on health and safety matters for those teaching science in primary schools and similar establishments, such as nursery schools, some middle schools and some schools for children of secondary age with special educational needs. It also covers the curriculum areas, in the same establishments, variously known as design and technology (in England and Wales) or technology/technologies (in Northern Ireland and Scotland), which we collectively call 'technology' in this book. A characteristic that distinguishes all such establishments from secondary schools is that science and technology is normally taught by non-specialists in non-specialist accommodation. However, in rare cases where primary schools have access to more specialist science or technology facilities, additional hazards can arise and these are considered in a new section, 19, *Taking it further*.

When we refer to 'children', this should be taken to include those aged from about 3 to 11 or 12. Thus those in nurseries are included as well as those in primary schools, and some in middle schools. Older children may also be included if their curriculum is closer to that commonly adopted in primary schools. Clearly, teachers will need to exercise their professional judgement in differentiating between activities suitable for 3-year-olds (perhaps with a good adult to child ratio) and those suitable for 11-year-olds in a class of 30. The presence of children with known health problems (e.g. allergies to food items, latex or pollen) or known behavioural problems will affect this judgement (see Section 2, *Risk assessment*).

We believe this book's coverage is sufficiently broad to encompass almost any science- or technology-based activities that might be found in primary schools. We hope the book will be used in schools throughout the UK and, indeed, more widely. We consider that its scope is wide enough to give writers or curriculum developers guidance on what might, or might not, be appropriate.

It is likely that all members of staff in a primary school will teach science and technology, sometimes as part of a topic- or theme-based approach. Practical activities and investigative work should form essential parts of much of this work. By its very nature, the best of investigative work does not lend itself to detailed prescription, not least as to the health and safety issues that may arise. The purpose of this book is, therefore, to provide general and wide-ranging information and advice. This should raise awareness of the hazards and risks that may be met in some of these practical activities and enable class teachers either to avoid such risks entirely or to control them adequately.

Safeguarding children

Children need to be encouraged to behave in ways that are safe to themselves and others and to develop an understanding of dangers and how to stay safe.

We do not wish to be alarmist; quite the reverse. Children are much safer in school than they are at home or when travelling between home and school. Within school, science is one of the safest activities – far more accidents occur in the playground or during PE lessons. Minor accidents which result in scratches, bumps and cuts are an acceptable part of growing up and a necessary part of the learning process. This book recognises and accepts that principle. It is written in an attempt to maintain the very good health and safety record of science by preventing significant avoidable injury.

Great health and safety myths

The myth Children are banned from throwing snowballs

The reality Every year we hear inaccurate stories about children who aren't allowed to throw snowballs, and swimmers who can't take their traditional winter dip in the local lake. All this in the name of health and safety.

If we spend time on the trivial risks there's a chance we'll miss the most important ones. We need to focus on finding ways for things to happen, not reasons to stop them – a sensible approach to managing risk focuses on practical action to tackle risks that cause real harm and suffering.

HSE

Go to www.hse.gov.uk/myth/index.htm to find out more   No 21 December 2008

Who is this book for?

- Teachers in nursery schools
- Teachers in primary schools (including infant, first and junior schools)
- Teachers in middle or preparatory schools
- Teachers in schools or units catering for children with special educational needs
- Teachers in secondary schools involved in primary liaison
- Nursery nurses, teaching assistants (TAs), higher level TAs (HLTAs) and classroom assistants
- Parents and others helping teachers in the classroom and outside
- Headteachers and science subject leaders or coordinators in the above schools
- Staff in field centres, museums and similar establishments
- Teachers in training
- Teacher trainers and INSET providers
- Employers, including (where relevant) education authorities and members of school governing bodies or school boards
- Anyone responsible for preparing model (general) risk assessments under various health and safety regulations
- Health and safety advisers, officers and consultants
- Science and/or technology advisers, inspectors and consultants
- Writers, curriculum developers and publishers
- Visiting scientists
- Equipment suppliers

Employers

This book frequently refers to the role of employers. The employer is the body with whom the employee has a written contract of employment. In schools this may be:

- local authorities in England and Wales (for community and voluntary-controlled schools);
- governing bodies in England and Wales (for foundation, trust and voluntary-aided schools and academies);
- education authorities in Scotland;
- education and library boards in Northern Ireland (these are due to be replaced by a single Education and Skills Authority but implementation has been delayed and is uncertain at the time of writing);
- governing bodies, charitable trusts or proprietors in independent schools.

Note on the fourth edition

This edition supersedes the third edition of *Be safe!* (2001). Although the general messages remain unchanged, there are many changes in detail, for example to improve clarity, because thinking has changed or the better to reflect government priorities. The book is longer and there are new sections on *Under-5s* and *Taking it further* (including primary/secondary liaison). The sections have been re-ordered and there is more emphasis on teaching health and safety through science and technology.

The ASE publishes the *Be safe! INSET Pack*, which is intended for use by science coordinators, headteachers, advisers, advisory teachers and teacher trainers to support both continuing professional development and initial teacher training. See Section 20, *Bibliography*.

This fourth edition of *Be safe!* has been welcomed by the following government education departments who commend it to teachers and others involved in primary science education:
- Northern Ireland Department of Education
- Scottish Government Education Department
- Welsh Assembly Government Department for Children, Education, Lifelong Learning and Skills

In England, inspectors of the Office for Standards in Education encourage its use.

Making a risk assessment simply involves a careful examination of what could cause harm to people and weighing up whether sufficient precautions are in place or whether more needs to be done to minimise harm. In most cases, in the primary school, a risk assessment is little more than common sense and prudent primary teachers do it informally as a matter of course.

A **hazard** is anything that might cause harm. For example, some microorganisms cause ill health and saws may cause personal injury. Hazards are not confined to science and technology: running in the corridor presents hazards as well.

The **risk** is the likelihood that a hazard will cause harm. This depends on how likely it is that something will go wrong, how serious an injury would result if it did and the number of people who might be affected. These will include other adults in the classroom, cleaners, visitors, etc. The experience of the person in charge of the class or group will affect the risk.

Control measures are the safety precautions adopted to reduce the risk, but the hazard will always be present. For example, kitchen and craft knives present an obvious hazard. The risk is reduced by keeping them locked away when not in use, teaching children to use them correctly and close supervision (see below) when they are using them.

The aim of risk assessment is to reduce the risks to as low a level as is reasonably practicable. Nothing in life is completely safe and we would not help children prepare for life outside school if we tried to wrap them in cotton wool and never did anything that presented a hazard. Children should be progressively introduced to ideas of hazard and risk and how to reduce the risks from hazards in their daily lives.

Ultimate legal responsibility for risk assessment rests with employers. Most education employers have adopted *Be safe!* as a collection of **model (general) risk assessments** for the primary phase. Teachers then have a duty to follow such advice, adapting it where necessary

to the particular circumstances of their schools and their children. Activities that might generally be considered safe enough with one age group may not be appropriate with children of a different age or who have special educational needs or disabilities. An experienced teacher may be better able to anticipate problems than a new entrant into the teaching profession. Equally, an activity appropriate for a Monday morning may be less so on a Friday afternoon or after a wet playtime, when behaviour may be a limiting factor. Overcrowding and/or large numbers may also make some activities unsafe.

A school, in drawing up its scheme of work, should incorporate the significant findings of risk assessment, which might include relevant points from *Be safe!* or elsewhere. This will not only draw them to the attention of teachers at the time they need to know it (when planning a lesson) but also help in the induction of new staff. Ideas for science activities obtained from books, magazines and the internet may not only be inappropriate, but also too dangerous. It is wise to assume that such activities may not be safe and will need a careful risk assessment.

If you haven't done it before, try it out first.

Close supervision is sometimes necessary. This means that a small group of children (up to about six) should have the undivided attention of the supervising adult. Such adults need not be teachers but, if they are parents, classroom assistants or other helpers, they must have been well briefed on the nature of the risk by the teacher in charge and be aware of guidance in *Be safe!* or elsewhere. Activities requiring close supervision of 7-year-olds may need less close supervision when carried out by 11-year-olds, although this will also depend on the maturity and behaviour of the class and the experience of the teacher or group leader. This is why it is important for teachers to know their children and exercise their professional judgement within the confines of the school's health and safety policy.

Immediate remedial measures

First aid can only be given by a qualified first-aider, but immediate remedial measures are things that an adult could be expected to do to help an injured child until first aid, a paramedic or an ambulance arrives. Where relevant, guidance on immediate remedial measures is given in this book.

An example of a risk assessment

The following example of a risk assessment is given in a little more detail than in the main text. We hope this will be useful to show how the more succinct comments in the text have been arrived at and the issues teachers need to consider before adopting particular control measures for an activity.

Using egg boxes

Paper pulp egg boxes are useful for model making and seed planting. They may be contaminated by the remains of broken eggs, chicken feathers and faeces. There are concerns about the hazard of food poisoning, such as that caused by salmonella.

However, the risk of this happening is low; eggs stamped with a little lion symbol come from chicken flocks that have been tested for salmonella. The risk can be made lower by the following control measures:

■ remind children to bring only clean egg boxes to school;

■ check for any contamination on the boxes and discard any dirty ones;

■ remind children to wash their hands after the activity. (This will be necessary anyway after working with glue, soil, paint, etc.) See Section 5, *Ourselves*.

This demonstrates that there is no reason for banning pulp egg boxes from school science and technology.

Making a safer world

Children grow up in a dangerous world. It is part of their education to learn how to approach hazards in a safe way. This process starts at home and continues throughout their schooling and for the rest of their lives.

All children need to be given clear guidance, rules and boundaries. The process of developing understanding begins with young children considering their own safety so they need to be encouraged to do this as early as possible by talking about why it is important to stay healthy and safe.

It is therefore valuable for teachers to talk to pupils about the safety needs of an activity and to guide them into thinking about their own approach to healthy and safe practice, both in the classroom and the wider world. Indeed, application to the wider world is particularly important as children's perception of risk is often heightened by how frightening or unfamiliar something is. For example, children often associate a high risk of harm with thunder and lightning although the risk indoors is actually very low.

Children also learn by observing good practice of adults and other children. Teachers must therefore always model good practice and insist that children follow their example.

Developing classroom practice

To develop an increasing awareness of the importance of staying healthy and safe, children need to be taught:

■ about the risks associated with their activities; and

■ how to carry out the activities safely.

Children could be asked to draw up their own safety codes for some activities. In this way they will begin to understand the reasoning behind the rules and practices. As they become older they develop greater awareness of others and of the impact of their actions upon them. Teachers can then guide and encourage children to suggest simple safety measures that apply to specific familiar activities. As children approach the end of their primary education they can be encouraged and expected to draw on earlier safety teaching to consider the health and safety implications of less routine practical activities which they plan for themselves.

In this way, children will be encouraged to:

■ independently identify hazards in activities undertaken; and

■ make and act on suggestions to control obvious risks to themselves and others.

Putting health and safety in context

The range and relevance of science and technology activities offer an excellent context in which to learn about and practise the knowledge and skills children need to be safe and can contribute to the development of a positive attitude towards safety. For example, see the guidance on hand-washing in Section 5, *Ourselves and our senses*.

Children should be encouraged to develop responsibility in the application of science and technology in relation to society and the natural environment. In their study of the local environment, children begin to appreciate how their actions can influence it for good or ill. Arising from their awareness of safety in their own environment, children should develop a concern for global issues which affect the safety and well-being of all living things.

Hazards of the internet

The internet and information technologies are useful tools for researching, collecting and analysing data in science and technology. However, this technology is open to abuse and can place children in danger. This concern is not restricted to science and technology; it is a whole-school matter which links to e-safety such as the use of mobile phones and cyber-bullying. Teachers should follow their school guidance.

Be safe! contains advice relevant to all activities for under-5s (i.e. foundation and/or early years) in science and technology. These activities provide a context for very young children to develop an awareness of their personal safety. They gain confidence, with suitable encouragement, to try new things and push the boundaries. But they may be unaware of the risks as they explore their world. Adults working with young children will find information in this book to give them the confidence to plan activities and enhance children's experiences. For some activities which are characteristic of foundation and early-years practice, you will find risk assessments in this section. Risk assessment for other activities, such as farm visits, keeping animals, cooking, making things and exploring household materials, which are less specific to this age group, are included in other sections of the book.

Sand and water

- Use only 'silver sand', not builders' sand, to avoid cuts and abrasions.
- If outside, sand and water trays must be covered when not in use to prevent fouling. Even so, carry out a quick visual check to ensure nothing has got underneath overnight.
- Keep the sand clean. Change water and sand regularly and clean the tray and toys. Clean condensation off the cover if it forms overnight.
- Site trays away from electrical equipment which may be damaged by sand or water.
- Teach children not to touch electrical equipment, such as a computer, with wet hands.
- If sand gets into the eyes, wash gently with clean water. Discourage rubbing.

Weather

Under-5s should be accustomed to moving between the indoor and outdoor classroom.

When planning outdoor activities for science and technology, remember to plan for the weather too. On hot days, use shaded areas if possible to carry out the activities, and consider doing them earlier, e.g. before 11.00 am. Schools normally have hot-weather guidance to help everyone to keep cool, which includes encouraging children to wear sun hats outside, drink more frequently and wear suitable sunscreen.

There is useful information and teaching resources for primary schools from Cancer Research UK (see Section 20, *Bibliography*).

Conversely, if you expect wet or cold weather, check that children know what clothing to bring to keep themselves warm and dry in the outdoor activity.

Gardening

Children in the foundation and early years may experience both structured gardening experiences and child-initiated digging and 'planting' play. This section should be read in conjunction with the more detailed information in the discussion on *Gardening* in Section 6, *Studies out of the classroom*.

Some points of particular concern to teachers of very young children are:

- the risk of seeds being put into ears, mouths, etc.;
- the suitability and size of tools;
- fouling, glass and other dangerous litter in the soil; and
- the need to wash hands afterwards.

Advice about poisonous and irritant plants can be found in Section 9, *Plants*.

Food

Hygiene with regard to food is especially important. Most primary school food preparation and cooking activities are suitable for very young children if they are very closely supervised and shown the correct way to do them, e.g. grating, cutting with a knife sharp enough for the task and melting butter or chocolate. See Section 7, *Food and hygiene*, for advice about cooking. Sections 8 (*Microorganisms*), 15 (*Glass and alternatives*) and 16 (*Heating and burning*) will also be relevant to some activities.

Food may also be used as a play material, e.g. in the sand or water tray or for more structured science investigations such as floating and sinking.

■ Teach children that food which is used for play should not be eaten.

■ Dry foods such as rice or uncooked pasta can be used for a longer time than cooked foods (such as cooked spaghetti), fruits, vegetables, jelly, etc.

■ Food used for play should be disposed of as kitchen waste.

For advice on investigating foods and other kitchen materials such as detergents, see Section 17, *Chemicals*.

Make yourself aware of any children with food allergies before planning activities involving food. Warn parents if you are planning activities with novel foods such as kiwi fruit.

Example of a risk assessment

Children explore forces using toys that move, such as bikes, scooters and cars.

Hazards include:

■ damaged toys, possibly leading to cuts;

■ children not knowing how to operate toys safely, possibly leading to bruises, sprains and grazes if they fall off; and

■ children colliding with other children or obstacles, possibly leading to cuts and bruises.

The likelihood of injury is quite high, because children enjoy using toys and may ignore faults or use them without enough care or awareness of others, although the injuries are usually not serious, so the **risk of serious injury** is low. The **control measures (precautions)** to reduce the risks are:

■ good maintenance of the toys, with damaged ones being removed from use;

■ teaching children about safe use, including awareness of others;

■ designating areas for use of moving toys; and

■ limiting the number of children using moving toys at any one time.

Building things

Under-5s will learn about forces, materials and cutting and joining through activities such as modelling with recycled and natural materials and using construction kits.

■ Teach children not to lift items that are much too big or heavy for them.

■ Teach children how to lift items safely: bend knees, keep back straight, grip securely, keep what is being lifted close to the body.

■ Check that recycled materials, such as cardboard boxes, other packaging and wood brought from home, are clean and have no sharp edges, protruding staples, splinters, etc. See also the risk assessment for the use of egg boxes in Section 2, *Risk assessment*. There have

been unsubstantiated concerns raised about using toilet roll centres: they can be used if they are checked in the same way as egg boxes, or use kitchen roll centres.

■ Some construction kits contain very small components and are unsuitable for this age group.

■ If working with very large-scale construction kits, only allow children to climb or ride on what has been constructed after testing by the teacher or support staff. This ensures that it is sturdy enough to carry them safely.

Further advice about making things and, for example, the safe use of tools can be found in Section 12, *Making things*.

Big apparatus

Through playing on big apparatus, children learn about their bodies and experience the effects of forces.

■ Ensure apparatus is installed on a suitable surface.

■ Be aware that, when wet, some materials and surfaces become too slippery for safe use.

■ Teach children how to use apparatus safely, e.g. a slide, and to be aware of others, e.g. when on a swing rope.

SAFETY CODE when working with the under-5s

■ Regularly check that all toys and equipment are clean and serviceable, with no broken parts.

■ Ensure that toys and equipment, especially if borrowed from older year groups in the school or not obtained from an educational supplier, are suitable for this age group.

■ Store anything which children use at an accessible height. Children should not stretch or climb to reach it.

■ Teach (and supervise) correct hand-washing techniques. See the discussion on *Looking after ourselves* in Section 5, *Ourselves and our senses*.

■ Some footwear, e.g. flip-flops, may be unsuitable for active play such as using moving toys and big apparatus, or for building and gardening activities.

■ Young children should not blow up balloons because of the risk of choking.

Children are interested in, and should know something about, themselves. They will gain an understanding of biological variation through a study of individual differences. Although, in general, this is thought of as a 'safe' topic, there are some aspects where there are possible hazards.

Make sure that each child is physically fit for the activity that she or he is about to undertake. You should not investigate the effects of exercise on breathing or pulse rate, or carry out measurements of lung capacity, with children excused from PE on medical grounds.

Take care that children with medical problems (e.g. epilepsy, asthma, allergies to peanuts, etc.) are not put at risk. Follow your school's guidance concerning the keeping and giving of any medicines.

Avoid situations that can lead to emotional stress: investigations can change into competitions and some children may feel they are being identified as 'abnormal'.

Children in step-families and those who are adopted may be sensitive about the subject of heredity, and therefore this must always be approached with care.

SAFETY CODE for investigating ourselves

- Be sensitive to the differences between children.
- Avoid putting individuals into situations of physical or emotional stress.
- When investigating children's pulse rate, keep exercise to the same level as is normal in PE. Any equipment used must be robust and well maintained.
- Beware of using stairs for exercising. Teach children to hold the hand-rail.
- When smelling things, put them in a container covered with muslin or a lid with small holes so that they cannot be eaten by mistake (see Section 7, *Food and hygiene*).
- When foods are used for investigations into the sense of taste, ensure that all surfaces and utensils are clean and that children do not share spoons or cups. Whenever possible, use disposable items such as drinking straws to avoid sharing. Do not allow the foods to become contaminated and, before handling food, teach children to wash their hands and dry them hygienically, preferably using paper towels.
- Wash mouthpieces, dental mirrors and any other shared objects put into the mouth in warm soapy water and then disinfect them using Milton sterilising fluid or tablets (made up according to the manufacturer's instructions for babies' bottles), but remember that disinfection takes 15 minutes.
- Teeth should be sterilised as above before being handled by children.
- Disclosing tablets may be used safely and children should be taught how to use them properly.
- If measuring body temperatures on the forehead or under the armpit with re-usable sensors, follow the supplier's instructions regarding disinfection. Antiseptic wipes may be suitable. See the discussion on *Measuring temperature* in Section 16, *Heating and burning*.

Investigations on light and sound

- Teach children never to stare directly at any intense light source such as the Sun, a data projector, a laser pointer or a very bright torch.
- Children should not use laser pointers. They are also best avoided by teachers because, while class 1 and class 2 lasers should be safe and so marked, the labelling is not always reliable.
- Light-emitting diodes (LEDs) are not the same as laser diodes and items such as LED torches, available from reputable suppliers, can be used safely by children. Wind-up LED torches are particularly useful for showing simple energy transfers.
- For most people with epilepsy, a seizure will not be brought on by a flashing light. If in doubt, a person with epilepsy should simply look away.
- When working in dark areas, ensure floors are uncluttered and be alert to some children's fear of the dark.
- Warn children never to poke anything into their ears (or other body orifices).
- When doing work on sound and hearing, warn children not to shout or blow down speaking tubes.

- See also the *Safety code to avoid looking at the Sun* in Section 6, *Studies out of the classroom*.
- If you want to carry out cheek-cell sampling, see Section 19, *Taking it further*.

Looking after ourselves

From foundation and early years onwards, it is essential that children are taught the importance of looking after themselves, including maintaining good hygiene and keeping healthy.

Washing hands properly is fundamental to good hygiene and will enable children to avoid many of the hazards and risks which might be associated with science or technology activities. Hand-washing is mentioned in a number of the sections of this book and it is important that children are taught how to wash their hands properly. The safety code for hand-washing provides good guidance for teachers. The *Safety code for maintaining good hygiene: hand-washing* can be downloaded as a poster from the ASE website at http://www.ase.org.uk/resources/health-and-safety-resources/health-and-safety-primary-science/

Note that alcohol gel may be useful in some contexts but is not a substitute for good hand-washing with warm water and soap.

You may find the rhyme below, sung to the tune of the *Hokey Cokey*, helps younger children to learn and practise washing their hands carefully. If sung at a reasonable pace, it will take 25 seconds.

> *You put your right hand in and your left one too,*
> *You get a load of soap and you rub them through and*
> *through,*
> *You go between the fingers and you twist your hands*
> *around,*
> *That's what you have to do!*
> *Oh ... we're washing our hands* (repeat 3 times)
> *Rinse and dry and now you're nice and clean again.*

SAFETY CODE for maintaining good hygiene: hand-washing

Teach children to wash their hands thoroughly and carefully.

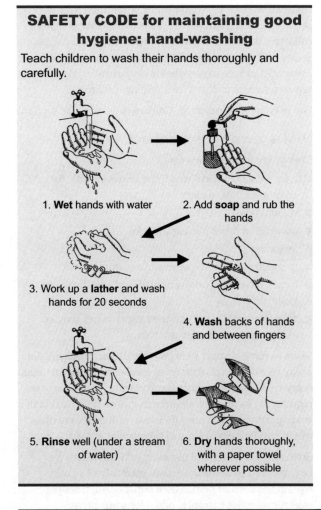

1. **Wet** hands with water

2. Add **soap** and rub the hands

3. Work up a **lather** and wash hands for 20 seconds

4. **Wash** backs of hands and between fingers

5. **Rinse** well (under a stream of water)

6. **Dry** hands thoroughly, with a paper towel wherever possible

Teach children:

- how 'germs' spread;
- about the need for careful washing of surfaces and utensils (e.g. in food preparation or microbiology);
- about the need to use tissues after sneezing and to wash their hands afterwards;
- that staying healthy requires a balanced diet;
- about the need for taking sufficient exercise;
- that listening frequently to loud sounds can damage their hearing;
- about the dangers of looking at the Sun, directly or through lenses, coloured glass, optical instruments, etc. (See the *Safety code to avoid looking at the Sun* in Section 6, *Studies out of the classroom*);
- about the dangers of mains electricity (see Section 14, *Teaching about electricity and using electrical equipment*); and
- about the hazards of many household chemicals (see Section 17, *Chemicals*).

All of these can be taught as part of science activities.

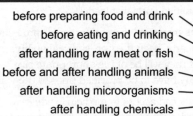

WASH YOUR HANDS

before preparing food and drink
before eating and drinking
after handling raw meat or fish
before and after handling animals
after handling microorganisms
after handling chemicals

after going to the toilet or blowing your nose
after pond dipping
during farm visits, before eating
after handling plants
after handling soil (check fingernails)
after working outdoors

Environmental areas

Environmental areas offer opportunities for children to study aspects of the environment at first hand. They may also be involved in maintaining the school environmental area, which may or may not contain a pond. Careful planning and management can enable a school to create various types of environment (marsh, rocks, etc.), allowing children to investigate and to follow seasonal changes, which are impossible during a single off-site visit.

Supervision outdoors is different to that in the classroom and children must be effectively supervised even for short activities within the school grounds. Follow national/local guidance and your school's policy for organising and running off-site visits.

Environmental visits present excellent opportunities to teach children about common hazards such as uneven ground, trips and slips, hazardous litter, animal faeces, brambles and similar plants. Be particularly alert to the dangers of children falling into ponds or wandering out of sight. More-detailed advice on the use of ponds can be found in the *Safety code* in this Section and on their creation at http://www.ase.org.uk/resources/health-and-safety-resources/health-and-safety-primary-science/

Cuts on exposed skin present a risk of tetanus from soil but the risk is low because most children receive tetanus vaccination as part of the UK NHS childhood immunisation programme. Weil's disease is a similar risk from ponds (and surrounding vegetation) polluted by animal urine, although it is rare in the UK. Nevertheless, make sure that cuts and abrasions are covered by waterproof plasters before pond-dipping. Check whether there is a risk of Lyme disease (from ticks) in your area (see Section 20, *Bibliography*, for NHS Direct).

In all environmental studies, every consideration should be given to avoid damaging the environment and disturbing the balance of animal and plant populations. The removal of fossils, minerals or rocks should only be done after due consideration and with permission. The removal of plant material without the landowner's permission may also be an offence. For a number of protected species of plants, collecting the whole or parts (e.g. the flower) of those plants is illegal. If the planned activity involves children turning over rocks or logs to see what is underneath, ensure they are replaced carefully in their original position.

See also the discussion on *Gardening* later in this section.

Visits away from school

These may include visits to:

- a forest school, local wood, the seashore, etc., for environmental studies;
- national parks;
- quarries or other industrial sites;
- factories;
- museums, including open-air museums;
- farms, whether working or designed specifically for visits; and
- zoos or animal sanctuaries where children may be able to get very close to animals.

Visits to more-distant sites pose particular problems not always encountered when using local environmental areas. A prior visit by the teacher is recommended and may be required by local rules. Centres that have their own staff leading activities will have their own risk assessments, which can be helpful for staff preparing for a visit.

Such visits need careful planning and should always be organised in accordance with your school's policy regarding parental permission, supervision, transport, safety, first aid, insurance, and – for some areas – competent and qualified specialist leaders.

Children and adults may need to wear particular protective clothing and footwear. Check their on-site availability, and especially that they will be of the appropriate size. Otherwise, they may have to be provided prior to the visit.

Some children may need access to medicines while participating in outdoor studies. The administration of medicines, whether prescription or non-prescription, needs to follow the same safety principles that apply in school. It is important to follow your school guidance. The governments in the UK have produced booklets that give sound guidance (see Section 20, *Bibliography*).

> Schools will probably have an educational visits coordinator. Further information is available from government departments, the Health and Safety Executive (HSE) and articles in *Primary Science* (see Section 20, *Bibliography*).

Farm visits

Farm visits offer great educational opportunities. The main hazards are likely to be posed by the unwitting transfer of microorganisms to the visitors. This can be controlled by effective hygiene, which, in the main, means frequent and careful hand-washing during the visit and before any eating and drinking (or thumb-sucking, etc.). Certain strains of *E. coli* have caused problems in recent years but the risks from these can be managed through good hygiene. Children must be sufficiently supervised to ensure that they maintain this hygiene.

FEED THE ANIMALS

Forest schools

Forest school types of outdoor activities often include campfires and tree climbing. Before undertaking such activities, consult trained practitioners for risk assessments.

SAFETY CODE for studies out of the classroom

In addition to the points mentioned below, the *Safety codes* for animals, plants and microorganisms also apply.

■ Children (and adults) must wash their hands thoroughly whenever they have handled or examined animals, plants, soil, pond water, etc. When working outdoors, if soap and water are not available, ensure that children's hands are cleaned with wipes or gels before eating or drinking anything. Otherwise, discourage eating the sweets and other snacks that children carry with them.

■ Cover cuts and abrasions with waterproof dressings. Take a supply with you.

■ Be prepared for stings from wasps, bees, jellyfish, nettles, etc. In some cases, these may need first aid treatment.

■ Children who have medical conditions may need access to their medication while off-site. Follow your school's guidance on the administration of medicines.

■ Consider the clothing needs according to season. Ensure children's exposed skin is protected from sunlight with long sleeves and/or sunscreen, and that hats are worn. Children often become absorbed in their work, shedding hats or coats and failing to notice the effects of the Sun, or even cold.

■ Ensure adequate footwear if there is the danger of slipping on wet grass, rocks and seaweed, etc.

■ Check for the presence of hazards such as broken glass, cat/dog fouling, irritant or poisonous plants, wasp nests, etc.

■ Only allow children to climb rocks and trees within their capabilities and with supervision.

■ Clearly define the area within which the children should remain.

■ If working on the seashore, take proper account of the local tide patterns.

■ Children should wear eye protection when chipping rocks.

■ Pooters should have separate mouthpiece tubes which can be disinfected (e.g. in Milton sterilising fluid or tablets, made up according to the manufacturer's instructions for babies' bottles) before and after being put in the mouth.

■ Be careful about handling or eating crops which may have been sprayed with fertilisers and pesticides.

■ Hands should be protected by disposable gloves or plastic bags if litter is collected for surveys.

For ponds

■ Cover cuts and abrasions with waterproof plasters before pond-dipping.

■ Do not allow unrestricted access to ponds or allow young children to work unaccompanied.

■ Teach older children how to work around a pond unaccompanied by an adult and without endangering themselves or others. Do not, however, allow this unless you can be reasonably certain of their sensible behaviour. In any event, the teacher should always be near enough to respond in an emergency.

■ Avoid pond-dipping where access is steep or otherwise difficult.

■ Avoid open water (i.e. unfenced water) which could be deep and dangerous.

■ See Section 20, *Bibliography*, for more detailed advice about ponds.

For farm visits

■ Ensure children wash their hands frequently, and certainly before eating, drinking, thumb-sucking, etc.

■ Warn children to be very careful with barbed wire, electric fences or any fences which may be contaminated by animals.

■ Women who are, or might be, pregnant should avoid farm visits during lambing time. This should be covered by a pregnancy risk assessment.

To avoid looking at the Sun

■ Teach children that they should never look at the Sun directly or through a lens or coloured glass.

■ Eclipses, or sunspots, may be safely viewed by projection. Even during an eclipse, the direct light from the Sun can permanently damage the eye.

■ Be especially careful when looking through binoculars or telescopes not to look at the Sun accidentally.

■ Do not leave lenses, magnifying glasses, bottles of water or broken glass in positions where they may focus sunlight and cause a fire.

■ When using a microscope that does not have a built-in light source, do not direct the mirror towards the Sun. This could reflect the light through the microscope and into the user's eye.

Gardening

Growing plants in a school garden fulfils a range of educational aims.

- It can start children thinking about where their food actually comes from.
- It can be used to teach about sustainability, and recycling in nature.
- It provides another opportunity to break the routine of school life and gives children a further opportunity to explore their environment.

School gardens need not be the size of allotments. They can be any size or simply comprise a group of containers or tubs in the playground. To be successful, the children need to share in the responsibility for looking after and managing the growing. In this way, there is less likelihood of damage, inadvertent or deliberate. If the school grounds are not secure, think about whether the garden needs its own boundary fence.

SAFETY CODE for gardening

- Children working in a garden area must be properly supervised.
- Provide children with suitably sized gardening tools and teach them how to carry and use the tools safely.
- Avoid all potential manual handling injuries by ensuring children are provided with appropriately sized equipment, including wheelbarrows. Do not let children attempt to lift heavy items such as large bags of compost.
- Restrict cutting tools to secateurs and then for older children only. Teach them how to use these properly.
- Teach children to wear appropriately sized gardening gloves for work where there is a risk of irritation, abrasions or cuts to fingers and hands, such as when pulling up weeds.
- Children should not use undiluted chemicals such as pesticides or those which accelerate composting. Teach children how to apply fertilisers such as those used for tomatoes. Only use those chemicals which are available from garden centres or DIY stores. Always read the labels, including instructions for use.
- Teach children to wash food crops before eating them.
- Teach children to beware of the fouling of freshly worked soil by cats, dogs and other animals.
- Teach children to wash their hands after working in the garden.
- See the discussion on *Hazardous edible plants* in Section 9, *Plants*.

Composting

Gardening will always lead to surplus and unwanted plant material. Composting enables nutrients to be recycled back into the soil to promote new plant growth. In composting, a wide range of invertebrate animals and microorganisms collectively digest the plant material and turn it into a dark, rich-looking material which can be dug in to the garden. During the composting process, heat is produced and the inside of a compost heap can become hot. However, in a garden-sized compost heap, the temperature is unlikely to rise sufficiently to destroy some weed and other unwanted seeds but will speed up the breakdown of the vegetable matter. Compost should not produce an unpleasant smell, either during the process or in the end product. Foul-smelling compost heaps are unlikely to be composting properly. See Section 20, *Bibliography*.

Hazards of composting

Beware of the following hazards when composting:

- Heavy lifting when the compost heap is 'turned'.
- Accidental injury from tools used to turn the compost which may slip or fly out of inexperienced or unwilling hands.
- The release of huge numbers of microorganism spores which may provoke an asthma attack in susceptible individuals. Such an attack is not likely to be any different or worse than that provoked by a walk through a field and gardening texts rarely refer to it as an issue. Young children may be more susceptible, though, than adult gardeners.
- Be aware that a warm compost heap may attract vermin. Don't compost meat, cooked foods (including bread) or egg shells, which are especially attractive to vermin.

Working with food offers many opportunities for science and technology activities. Use this topic to teach the importance of cleanliness and personal hygiene. See also Sections 8 (*Microorganisms*), 16 (*Heating and burning*) and 17 (*Chemicals*).

Check whether your children are allergic to any foods. Just touching a peanut may trigger a reaction. Nut allergies are relatively common but there may well be children with other food allergies in a class.

Preparation

Before starting work with food, children should tie back long hair, wash their hands and cover any cuts or scratches on their hands with waterproof dressings (which should be blue for food preparation). Encourage children to wear aprons.

Check that children rewash their hands after breaks and visits to the toilet.

A special food-preparation table is ideal but, if a classroom table has to be used, clean it first with hot water and detergent. Children can then work on individual clean boards or mats. Alternatively, use a plastic table cover kept for this purpose.

Store equipment used in food preparation, including cutlery, in secure, clean conditions. Use it only for food preparation.

Ingredients

Particular foods can present problems. Red kidney beans must be cooked thoroughly to destroy the poisons in the outer coat (or use tinned cooked ones). Avoid skin and eye contact with the juice and seeds of chilli peppers. Cover spices used for 'sniff tests' with muslin. Cook eggs and raw meat thoroughly to avoid the risk of food poisoning.

Activities involving hot oil or boiling sugar are inappropriate with this age group.

Tasting foods

Investigations involving tasting should follow the same hygiene rules as for cooking.

Allow hot foods and drinks to cool sufficiently before tasting.

Storage

Only store small quantities of food in school. Use labelled, rodent-proof containers (e.g. ice cream or margarine tubs).

Store perishable foods in a clean refrigerator at the correct temperature (5 °C or below), keeping high-risk raw foods such as uncooked meats separately on a lower shelf or in sealed containers. If a freezer is used, it should be set to −18 °C. A fridge-freezer thermometer is useful as a check and as a teaching aid. Do not refreeze food.

Use a cool-box or cool-bag and an ice pack to carry food from a fridge to the preparation area if the food is not to be used immediately.

Equipment

When using a microwave oven, always refer to the manufacturer's instructions. Plates and utensils, etc., with metal parts or metal decoration can become extremely hot and cause serious burns when taken out of the oven. Metal parts can also cause arcing and may start a fire.

When locating a cooker, consider the fire risk to nearby flammable materials, such as curtains or displays, and the hazards associated with the movements of children. Any use of cookers, ovenware and food-processing equipment by children must be appropriately supervised. See also Sections 14 (*Electricity*) and 16 (*Heating and burning*).

Ideally, reserve a sink for washing up food utensils; if this is not possible, then at least keep a special washing-up bowl. A dishwasher is an effective alternative.

Although plastic utensils may appear attractive as being less hazardous, this is not always the case. Plastic knives are rarely effective and break easily and plastic graters do not work as well as metal ones.

SAFETY CODE for food hygiene

- Teach children the need for personal hygiene by means of food-preparation and tasting investigations.
- Ensure that food-preparation surfaces and utensils are clean.
- Use knives which are sharp, and teach children how to use them safely.
- Separate raw meats, fish and eggs from ready-to-eat foods such as fruit, bread and cooked meats.
- Use separate equipment for the preparation of raw meat/fish and ready-to-eat foods (i.e. foods that are already cooked or food that is eaten raw). Consider using colour-coded chopping boards (see suppliers' catalogues).
- Wash hands between handling raw meat/fish and ready-to-eat foods.
- Use cookery aprons, cooking utensils and washing-up equipment for food preparation only.
- Site cookers carefully and maintain them according to the manufacturers' instructions.
- Be aware that some people have medical (e.g. allergies or diabetes), religious or cultural reasons for refusing to handle or eat certain foods (including additives). You should already be aware if this applies to any children in your class.
- Store food correctly and take note of the 'use-by' date.
- Dispose of surplus food materials through the kitchen waste system or via a compost bin. See the discussion on *Composting* in Section 6, *Studies out of the classroom*.

The term microorganisms (microbes) includes bacteria, fungi, algae, viruses and protoctista. However, the microorganisms' activities that are likely to be studied in primary schools are limited to simple investigations with less-harmful moulds, yeast and some bacteria. It is important always to apply safe and hygienic techniques when dealing with microorganisms of any type, since this will help to foster good practice.

Risks when using microorganisms

During the primary years, the emphasis will be on observation and carrying out simple investigations only.

Many microbes release large quantities of spores into the air. Some people are allergic to these and therefore microbes should be grown in securely covered containers, which are not opened. However, since yeasts produce large amounts of carbon dioxide gas as they grow, it is important that vessels containing fermenting yeasts are not completely sealed. A plug of cotton wool will allow the release of gas but will prevent any cells or spores from escaping or entering.

Spores may be produced when composting (see Section 6, *Studies out of the classroom*).

It is neither necessary nor advisable to grow microorganisms, often referred to as cultures, on special growth media such as agar.

It would be possible to grow a wide variety of potentially harmful microorganisms and the appropriate conditions for the safe handling of these are not likely to be found in primary schools. Any school contemplating this type of work with microorganisms should see Section 19, *Taking it further*.

Making yoghurt

Yoghurt-making provides an excellent example of developing children's scientific knowledge and understanding in a familiar domestic context. It may contribute to both their science and their technology education in a situation where they can themselves begin to understand the hazards, assess the risks and take appropriate action to reduce the risks. The main hazard is the possibility of contamination of the yoghurt by bacteria other than yoghurt species, leading to the risk of ill health. The risk can be reduced by treating the yoghurt as you should treat any food intended for human consumption (see Section 7, *Food and hygiene*).

Prevent contamination of the yoghurt by keeping it covered as much as possible and using only equipment kept for food preparation. If possible, use a proper yoghurt maker, thoroughly cleaned before use. Make the yoghurt using UHT milk and only open the cartons immediately before use.

Examples of suitable material

baker's yeast
hay or grass infusion in rainwater
mildews and rusts on weeds and garden plants
milk
edible mushrooms
mouldy cheese, bread or fruit
pond material
soil
yoghurt

A mould garden, using moist bread in a closed plastic bag that is punctured by a few pinpricks, may be used to show the variety of moulds. Alternatively, the bread may be put in a large screw-top jar with the lid fitted loosely. Disposal of such material needs special care – see *Safe disposal of microorganisms*.

SAFETY CODE for using microorganisms

- In all work with microorganisms, ensure adequate supervision and do not carry out the work with children who, given the level of supervision available, cannot reasonably be relied upon to follow instructions.
- Grow cultures of microorganisms only on the natural substances where they normally grow.
- It demonstrates good practice to wipe up all spills with disinfectant. However, for low-risk microbes such as those in yoghurt, yeast and milk, mop up with a dry paper towel and finish with hot water and detergent using a disposable cloth.
- Spills of hay infusion water should be treated with disinfectant. See *Safe disposal of microorganisms*.
- Securely close (but do not seal) all containers in which microorganisms are grown. Do not uncover them for clearer observation.
- Never allow fermentation by yeasts in sealed containers because the pressure of the gas generated could cause an explosion.
- Label (including the date) all cultures that are to be left for extended periods of study.
- Dispose of cultures as soon as possible after the activity.
- Promptly dispose of anything that begins to smell unpleasant.
- Never use material from dustbins, toilets or polluted water for investigations on microorganisms.
- Never attempt to grow cultures from anything produced by the body, including through coughs, sneezes or body orifices.

- If considering sampling from unwashed hands, etc., see Section 19, *Taking it further*.
- Cover all cuts and abrasions with waterproof plasters.
- Because of the possibility of contamination, teach children to wash their hands thoroughly with soap and water after handling any source of microorganisms.
- Teach children not to put anything into their mouths unless, of course, the microbes are in a food product, such as yoghurt, bread or some cheeses, which was made under hygienic conditions (see Section 7, *Food and hygiene*).

BIOHAZARD

Safe disposal of microorganisms

Yeasts, yoghurt and other foods not used for the study of decay should be treated as in Section 7, *Food and hygiene*.

Although not good laboratory practice, mouldy food, yeasts and yoghurt in closed containers may be disposed of as kitchen waste by placing the unopened container in the dustbin normally used for the school refuse.

All other cultures, such as hay infusions, must be disposed of as described below.

- Cultures should be sterilised prior to disposal. The most effective method involves heating for 15 minutes in a pressure cooker. Because primary schools are unlikely to have a pressure cooker, the next best alternative is to use disinfectant.
- Always use a freshly prepared solution of disinfectant. *Virkon* is very suitable and available in 50 g sachets from suppliers such as Philip Harris. Follow the instructions for making up the solution. Bleach is a less satisfactory alternative, because the concentration of ordinary bleach is unknown and bleach is quickly broken down by organic matter. However, if bleach is to be used, buy a good-quality domestic brand (the bottle should be labelled irritant) and dilute with no more than nine times its volume of water, aiming for a 10% solution or stronger. Wear gloves when handling all solutions of disinfectant.
- While wearing gloves, open the culture of microorganisms under the surface of the disinfectant, e.g. in a bucket, so as not to release live spores into the air. Soak the culture for at least one hour, or overnight.
- Pour away the disinfectant, place the culture in an opaque polythene bag and put this in the dustbin.
- Glass or other re-usable containers, after soaking in disinfectant, can be washed thoroughly with hot water and detergent and recycled.
- Keep disinfectant powders or solutions (including bleach) locked away until required.

Plants offer an easy opportunity for children to experience the wonder of watching a living organism grow and develop. By growing plants in the classroom, children can be encouraged to care for and appreciate the needs of other living organisms and to develop caring attitudes towards them.

When using garden soil, ensure that it is free from broken glass and is taken from a site unlikely to have been contaminated with the faeces of animals, especially cats and dogs. These animals are often sources of parasites.

SAFETY CODE for using plants

- Teach children to avoid touching their eyes whilst handling plants.
- Teach children never to taste any part of a plant unless they are absolutely certain that it is safe to do so.
- Warn children about attractive-looking fruits and seeds, especially those that look like edible ones but might be poisonous.
- Check whether seeds have been treated with pesticides. Teach children never to eat these.
- Always wash hands after handling plants, seeds or soil.
- Wear gardening or disposable gloves when working with plants known to be irritant.
- Do not use soil which is likely to be contaminated.

Seeds

Seeds from commercial growers may have been treated with poisonous pesticides (before buying, read the packet carefully). If you use treated seeds, ensure if possible that they can be scattered from the packet (e.g. lobelia and lettuce) or planted using tweezers (e.g. nasturtium), or wear plastic gloves. Seeds that are not treated with pesticide are available as food products from supermarkets and health-food shops.

Examples of suitable plants

These lists are only illustrative and do not preclude growing other species.

Plants for general use

begonia
busy Lizzie
coleus
fuchsia
garden herbs (e.g., chives, sage, mint)
geranium
Mimosa pudica (sensitive plant)
mother-of-thousands
pelargonium
philodendron
piggyback plant
rubber plant
spider plant
Swiss cheese plant
tradescantia

Plants with particularly interesting growth forms

bromeliads
cacti (be particularly careful with those forms having sharp spines)
succulents
carnivorous plants

Plants to illustrate growth from seeds

barley
broad bean
cress
dwarf bean
grass
maize
mung bean
mustard
oat
pea
radish
runner beans
sunflower
wheat

Various seeds and 'pips' from edible fruits including:

avocado
date
lemon
mango
orange

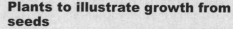

Hazardous plants

Even if a plant is known to be hazardous, it does not necessarily mean that it must be avoided, particularly when many are commonplace, e.g. privet and holly. What is important is the planned activity and the age, maturity and level of supervision of the children. It is important that children learn about the nature of plants in the exploration of their environments. To start with, it is a good idea to regard all plants, fungi and parts thereof as hazardous until you have certain knowledge to the contrary. Identification may require reference to suitable texts, such as *Poisonous plants and fungi in Britain* (see Section 20, *Bibliography*).

 Poisonous plants

The hazard is that the plants contain toxic chemicals. The risk is that the children may consume parts of the plant; this is most likely with seeds and fruits. If you bring these into the school environment, make sure that the children have no opportunity to eat them. Poisonous plants are acceptable in a supervised, gated wildlife area but not on the edge of such sites where children may have access from less closely supervised areas or out of school hours.

These plants – and all of their parts unless otherwise noted – should be considered poisonous:

black nightshade
castor oil seeds
henbane
holly
laburnum
privet
ragwort

black
bryony

red kidney beans (except when well cooked)
rowan seeds
spindle tree
yew
white bryony
woody nightshade

cuckoo pint

hemlock

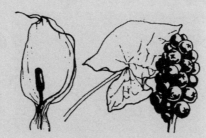

deadly
nightshade

Hazardous edible plants

- Although potatoes and tomatoes are good plants to grow in a garden, the leaves and stalks contain a poison and must not be eaten. This poison can be in any green parts of potato tubers but green tomatoes are safe to eat.
- Rhubarb leaves are poisonous but the stalks are edible.
- Chilli plants are best avoided because the chilli peppers contain substances which can be extremely hazardous to eyes.

Irritant plants

By touch

Several plants can cause irritation of the skin or dermatitis if they are touched. Examples are given below.

- Stinging nettles.
- Plants of the primrose family and goose grass (cleavers) may produce an allergic rash in some children.
- Giant hogweed (and other members of the Umbelliferae family); exposure to the Sun after touching the plant may result in burn-like lesions and blistering.
- Certain bulbs and corms of the lily family, such as hyacinth, bluebell and tulip, can cause contact dermatitis.

If you want pupils to work with any of these plants then plastic gloves or bags must be worn.

From pollen

- Grasses, catkins and many other plants produce wind-borne pollen which can cause hay fever and trigger an asthma attack. Avoid working with these plants *inside* the classroom if there is a risk of the release of large amounts of pollen.

Living things make an important contribution to the education of children. It is essential that all animals are well maintained. There must always be proper planning for their correct care and maintenance, including the potential difficulties of weekends and holiday times.

Check that none of the children in the class has a serious known allergy to animals or their bedding.

Teach children to handle all animals with due care. This includes specimens temporarily removed from the wild for study. Breeding pairs should not be kept unless there is someone in the school with the knowledge and commitment to ensure the care of both young and parent animals.

- Any animals taken from their natural environment for study should be returned as soon as possible.
- See Section 20, *Bibliography*, for guidance on keeping particular species.

Advice about particular animals

Frog and toad spawn

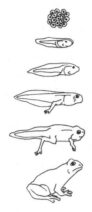

Take only small amounts of frog or toad spawn for study and provide suitable conditions for the tadpoles to grow and mature. (A tank 30 × 20 × 20 cm should be large enough to house 10–20 tadpoles). When observations are complete, return the animals into a suitable environment, preferably where the spawn was found. When legs appear, tadpoles become carnivorous and may eat each other if meat is not provided (uneaten meat needs to be removed daily). See Section 20, *Bibliography*.

Farm animals

When planning to rear farm animals which will ultimately be sent for slaughter, consider carefully the potential responses of the children (and their parents) and staff, and how the activity meets the curricular, cultural and ethical aspirations of the school.

Incubating eggs

Where hens', or similar, fertile eggs are incubated, prior arrangements must be made for the longer-term husbandry and welfare of the hatched birds. After handling chicks or ducklings, make sure that children immediately wash their hands. Fertile eggs should not be opened up merely to examine embryos.

Butterflies and moths

Some butterfly and moth larvae can be kept, where their food plant is available. Where possible, adults of native forms should be released in the area in which the larvae were found.

Small mammals

Note that the smaller mammals are less suitable for use in infant classrooms, since the children may have difficulty in handling them with care.

Honey bees

It is a good idea to encourage bees (and butterflies) with suitable planting. However, keeping bees in schools is not straightforward and should only be attempted if you have made contact with the British Beekeeping Association. See Section 20, *Bibliography*.

Examples of suitable animals

Amphibians
axolotls
spawn of common frog and toad
tiger salamanders

Birds
chickens and ducks

Invertebrates
brine shrimps
butterfly and moth larvae (but not caterpillars that are very hairy, which can cause skin rash)
chafer beetles
common pond creatures
earthworms
giant millipedes
hissing cockroaches
mealworm beetles
slugs and snails, including giant African land snails
stick insects (most)
woodlice

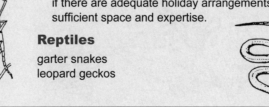

Fish
cold-water fish
tropical fish

Mammals
guinea pigs
Mongolian gerbils
rabbits
rats
Syrian hamsters (but note that they are nocturnal)

Smaller farm animals
Animals such as sheep and goats may be suitable if there are adequate holiday arrangements and sufficient space and expertise.

Reptiles
garter snakes
leopard geckos

SAFETY CODE for keeping and studying animals

- Adults and children should always wash their hands before and after handling animals and after replenishing or cleaning wild bird feeders and bird boxes.

- Obtain animals, particularly small mammals, only from reputable suppliers.

- Keep the housing clean and disinfect cages at regular intervals.

- Surfaces such as tables on which animals have been studied should be cleaned immediately afterwards with hot water and detergent.

- Where animals require fresh food, remove any uneaten surplus before it begins to decompose.

- To avoid the transmission of disease, prevent any contact between maintained animals or their foodstuffs and wild animals.

- Encourage children not to bring mammals and birds found in the wild, dead or alive (often injured), into school.

- For injured animals, consult animal welfare organisations such as PDSA (People's Dispensary for Sick Animals), RSPCA (Royal Society for the Prevention of Cruelty to Animals), SSPCA (Scottish Society for the Prevention of Cruelty to Animals) or a local vet.

- Avoid the possibility of children contaminating footwear or other clothing with animal or faecal material and bringing it into the classroom. Ensure any such contamination is cleaned up promptly.

- Do not allow animals to wander unrestricted around classrooms.

- Inform parents in advance if animals are to be brought into the classroom and check for possible allergies.

- Ask owners of cats and dogs brought into school for a short visit to confirm the pets are well behaved and free from disease and parasites.

- Ask owners to confirm that animals brought into school by a visiting animal scheme are well looked after and free from stress and disease.

Dealing with animal bites and scratches

- All animal scratches and bites should be treated by a first-aider.

- Seek medical advice if in doubt about the risks of infection.

 ## Animals which, in general, should not be kept

- **Any animals for which there is insufficient expertise, time, resources or commitment to ensure their well-being.**

- **Animals that can transmit diseases to humans, e.g.**
  mammals and birds caught in the wild.

- **Animals that it is illegal to take from the wild, e.g.**
  great crested newts; and
  natterjack toads.

- **Animals that may infest, e.g.**
  European or American species of cockroaches.

- **Animals that are venomous, e.g.**
  Florida striped stick insects;
  some snakes; and
  many tropical spiders (but note that, with care, some tarantulas are perfectly acceptable).

- **Animals that can cause allergic reactions, e.g.**
  locusts;
  garden tiger moth caterpillars (larvae); and
  brown-tailed moth caterpillars (larvae).

- **Animals that grow too big, e.g.**
  terrapins; and
  bullfrog tadpoles (the large adults must not be released into the wild and may be difficult to maintain).

- **Animals that require UV light, e.g.**
  many lizards.

- **Animals that are difficult to keep in the primary classroom, e.g.**
  exotic mammals; and
  birds (because they are noisy, messy and may transmit diseases or cause allergies).

Animal parts

It is both permissible and safe to study whole fish and offal – hearts, kidneys, etc. – but always obtain them fresh from a butcher, abattoir or fishmonger since the animals from which they have been taken will have been inspected and passed as fit for human consumption. You are unlikely to be able to obtain eyes of sheep, cows or goats easily but pigs' eyes are available. Materials from butchers will be safe to handle and cut up.

Be aware that some children may dislike handling parts of animals, and others may have cultural or ethical reasons for not wanting to do so. No pressure should ever be exerted on children to take part in these activities. Parts of animals should always be handled with sensitivity to their living origin.

If you are studying animal lungs, inflate them only with a bicycle or foot pump through tubing inserted into the windpipe, not by blowing with your mouth. It is sensible to enclose the lungs in a plastic bag to avoid tiny droplets of fluid (carrying microbes) being blown into the air.

When studying animal organs, cover the table with paper or a bin liner and dispose of it with the remains in sealed, opaque bags using the system the school kitchen uses. It might be more convenient to do the activity on a plastic tray.

Models of skeletons or body organs can sometimes provide a useful alternative to using animal parts. Do not accept donations of real human skeletons or fetuses.

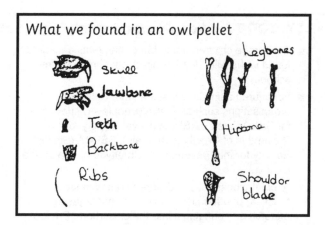

What we found in an owl pellet

Skull
Jawbone
Teeth
Backbone
Ribs
Legbones
Hipbone
Shoulder blade

SAFETY CODE for handling animal materials

- After the activity, wash equipment and surfaces with hot soapy water.
- Wash hands after handling any animal materials.
- Owl pellets can be dissected. They should be sterilised in a pressure cooker for 15 minutes before doing so. (Ask a local secondary school science department to do this for you.)
- Birds' nests must not be removed from the environment unless they are known to be no longer in use. Keep birds' nests, feathers, samples of sheep's wool, bones and unsterilised owl pellets found in the wild in sealed plastic bags or containers. Empty wasps' nests present fewer hazards.
- Dead mammals and birds are likely to be infected. They should not be brought into schools. However, if pupils do so, wrap the bodies in newspaper and a plastic bag and then dispose of as kitchen waste.

Instructions for adults to prepare animal bones for study, e.g. from a chicken

- With a sharp knife, remove as much flesh as possible. Place the bones in an old saucepan containing warm water with a small quantity of washing soda (sodium carbonate); you can buy this at your local supermarket or hardware store.
- Simmer (not boil) the bones until the remains of the flesh can easily be removed.
- Return the cleaned bones to the saucepan for a few more minutes and then use an old toothbrush to remove any remaining bits of meat.
- Rinse the bones in running water and place them in a bowl of water; add a good measure of undiluted domestic bleach (take care – see the discussion on *Dangerous chemicals* in Section 17, *Chemicals*) and leave until the next day. This will whiten and disinfect the bones.
- Remove the bones and allow them to dry; this can be accelerated by heating them gently in an oven.

In many science and technology activities, children make and test structures, mechanisms and other products. They might be working with wood, card, plastics, textiles, mouldable materials, components, etc. (for food, see Section 7, *Food and hygiene*). Teachers should choose tools that are appropriate to the materials and the maturity, experience and any special needs of the children. They should teach the correct use of tools such as scissors, craft knives and saws. Apart from being inherently good practice, this will stand the children in good stead in their activities outside school. Whenever tools are used, classroom management is of great importance.

Tools or materials donated by parents or industry, or brought in by teachers, may be unsuitable for school use and their acceptance and use should be considered carefully. Electrical items would need safety testing (see Section 14, *Teaching about electricity and using electrical equipment*).

SAFETY CODE for using tools and materials

- Make sure, by teacher demonstration, that children know how to use all the tools available to them.
- Generally, children should stand up when using saws, drills, hammers and craft knives as it is safer and more effective to do so.
- Teach children to keep the work area tidy by returning tools to the correct storage place, e.g. a trolley or board. Do not mount tool boards so high that children have difficulty reaching the tools.
- Teach children how to carry tools and materials safely.
- Consider providing for the needs of left-handed children, e.g. with special scissors or reversed bench hooks.
- Generally, most of the activities in primary school technology do not require safety spectacles (but see Section 19, *Taking it further*).
- Provide adequate space for each child and between children and make sure you can see what they are all doing.

Cutting

- Sharp tools are safer than blunt ones. Warn children to take care when using them. Use a cutting board secured with a clamp or a mat secured with masking tape.
- Children should use round-ended scissors unless the task requires pointed ones.
- Avoid the use of tin snips by children.
- Smooth or cover any sharp metal edges.

- Craft knives should only be used under close supervision and then only by responsible older children. They should use metal safety rules (rulers) for cutting in a straight line. Craft knives with retractable blades are strongly recommended but those with snap-off blades should not be extended beyond the first blade and snapping-off should be done by an adult. A 'quick-cutter' is a safer alternative for younger children.

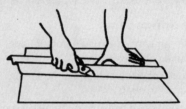

- Circle cutters require close supervision.
- Guillotines should only be used by adults. Trimmers are a safer alternative.
- Make sure that saw blades are firmly fixed to the handle and not bent. Secure the material firmly to the bench using a vice, bench hook or G-clamp.

- Expanded polystyrene can be cut safely with craft knives, scissors and hot-wire cutters (with good ventilation to get rid of the fumes). It should not be sanded.

SAFETY CODE for using tools and materials (continued)

Drilling holes

- Teach children to use a hole punch or paper drill when making holes in paper, card and corrugated plastic, and to use a cutting board or mat underneath. Do not use a pencil or screwdriver.
- Ensure hand drills (unless of the pistol-grip type) are used on a drill stand to promote safe, accurate working.
- If bradawls are used, close supervision is necessary.

Joining things

- Children rarely need to use hammers and, if they do, should use only small ones.
- Periodically check that hammer heads are firmly secured to the shaft.
- When hammering nails, hold the nail in a piece of plasticine or between the teeth of a comb.
- Teach children how to use staplers and staple guns safely. Close supervision is needed for staple guns.
- Although glues such as PVA are the most suitable for general woodworking and modelling, glue guns have their place. Low-melt glue guns, although less effective, are cooler and so safer (but will still burn). Hot-melt glue guns should only be used under close supervision and only by responsible older children. Use a glue gun stand.
- 'Super-glues' should not be used by children. Wallpaper pastes containing fungicide are also unsuitable.

- Glues which give off heavy vapours, such as impact adhesives, should only be used in a well-ventilated area. This includes spray adhesive, which, in addition, may be highly flammable. Make sure that there are no sources of ignition nearby. Spray adhesives should not be used by children.
- Beware of the risk of solvent abuse and of children becoming sensitised to adhesives. Follow manufacturers' instructions at all times.

Other tools and components

- Children should not use high-powered tools such as electric drills or jigsaws in the classroom, whether operated by mains electricity or rechargeable batteries (except model-making drills). For schools with access to workshop-type facilities, see Section 19, *Taking it further*.
- Soldering irons, if needed at all, should operate at low voltage, e.g. 24 volt. Always use low-fume solder (colophony-free or rosin-free) and work in a well-ventilated area. Use a stand for the iron.
- Avoid using wood chisels.
- When using balloons, balloon-powered toys, party blowers, etc., which are blown by mouth, teachers should observe hygienic procedures, and children should not share. For some applications, use of a balloon pump or plastic bottle to inflate the balloons is a better alternative.

- When using syringes in science and technology, teach children about the dangers of handling syringes and needles found outside the classroom.
- Young children need close supervision to ensure they do not eat or otherwise damage themselves with small objects such as beads, wood off-cuts or components from construction kits. Expanded polystyrene is best avoided with young children because it is so squashy. If inserted into ears or the nose, for example, it may require surgery for removal.

Finishing

- Fine dusts from wood and plastics are hazardous. However, manual sanding by small numbers of children for a short time is unlikely to produce dangerous levels of dust if adequate ventilation is provided.
- Be aware of the danger of sawdust being blown into the eyes.
- Spray paints and fixatives should only be used by adults and in a well-ventilated area.

SAFETY CODE for using textiles

- Needles and pins should be stored in a card or pin cushion. Make sure that all the needles and pins are returned to storage or returned with the work when the children finish the activity.
- Use the correct tools for the textile. Use the right size needles. Do not use fabric scissors for cutting anything else – they become blunt and will no longer cut fabric effectively.
- Keep threads short when hand-sewing so that the thread can be pulled through safely.
- Sewing machines can be used by older children with close supervision. They must be shown how to use the machine safely. Switch off the power at the wall socket before threading the needle. Sewing machines need to be serviced regularly.

Fabric irons

- Children should use irons only under close supervision. Set the ironing board at a suitable height and use lightweight irons, such as travel irons. Do not leave hot irons unattended by an adult.

Batik

- Use cold resists; rub on cold wax or wax crayon, or use starch or flour resists. If the children are mature enough to handle hot wax safely, the wax must be heated in a thermostatically controlled wax pot.

Dyeing

- Suitable dyes are:
  - natural dyes from edible plants such as beetroot juice, red cabbage, onion skins, tea, blackberries, blueberries or turmeric;
  - non-toxic, cold-water, domestic dyes;
  - food colouring; and
  - non-toxic fabric pens and paints.

Bleach

- Children should not use bleach.

SAFETY CODE for using mouldable materials

- In order to keep the material clean, children should ideally wash their hands before handling re-usable materials such as clay or salt dough or commercial cold-modelling materials such as Plasticine, Play-doh and Model Magic.

Plaster of Paris

- There are a variety of trade names under which plaster of Paris is sold. Mod Roc is the trade name of a bandage-like fabric impregnated with plaster of Paris. Plaster of Paris products become hot when mixed with water, particularly if the plaster of Paris is moulded in thick layers or shapes.
- Do not attempt to make a mould of a whole hand or encase any part of the body in plaster of Paris because it will cause serious heat burns.
- For making moulds, alginate gel is a safer, faster and cleaner material than plaster of Paris.

Vacuum forming

- Vacuum-forming equipment should only be used under close supervision in a well-ventilated area. The teacher should receive training before using this equipment.

Clay

- Wipe away any clay spilt on surfaces while it is still wet, to avoid dust.
- Avoid sanding dry clay.

Salt dough

- Salt dough is a low-risk material but warn children not to eat it.

Papier mâché

- To make papier mâché, use wallpaper paste that does not contain fungicide.

SAFETY CODE for ceramics

Kilns

- Kilns should only be operated by adults who have had training in how to use them safely and how to recognise faults. The kiln must be inspected regularly, including for electrical safety, by a qualified person.
- Fixed kilns should be in a caged-off area, with adequate space around the kiln and ventilation to remove the toxic fumes produced when firing.
- Kilns should have a door interlock, a temperature indicator and a clear ON indicator.
- Do not use fine silica such as ground flint for coating kiln furniture. Use a non-toxic batwash in slop form.
- Portable kilns need to be sited carefully in a secure area which children cannot access during firing. Firing is best done overnight; alert the caretaker when this is happening.

Glazes

- Purchase glazes as a liquid or a paste, not as a powder, and only from a reputable supplier.
- Only use non-toxic glazes.
- The glazes should be cookware quality regardless of what is being glazed.
- The glaze should be applied by dipping, pouring or brushing.
- Do not mix glazes or change their formulation (except glazes from a manufacturer's range designed to be mixed together).

Teaching about forces and motion, or related topics, may involve twisting, bending, stretching and squashing various materials. It may also involve work with magnets.

Magnets

Avoid using very small magnets with young children as they may put them into their mouths and swallow them.

Investigating magnetism may involve the use of iron filings. These become a nuisance when they stick on to magnets and may irritate the skin of younger children. They are particularly painful if they get into the eyes. Covering magnets with cling film and/or putting the filings in a sealed plastic bag or Petri dish will avoid many of the problems. Iron filings can be purchased in sealed plastic containers from many suppliers.

Strong magnets may 'jump' together quite violently and pinch the skin. They may also damage electronic circuits (including TV and monitor screens), watches and bank cards if brought near them or in contact with them.

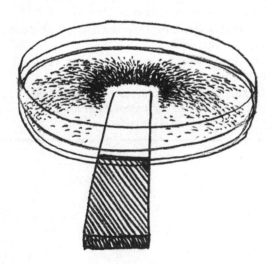

Testing things

Open-ended work often involves testing something the children have made, to see whether it works. Several topics require materials to be tested to breaking point.

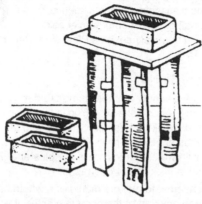

A key question for children (and their teachers) to ask is, if something breaks, where will everything (including you!) end up. Then take appropriate action to reduce the risk of harm when it does break.

Warn children about the possible dangers to faces, particularly to eyes, from rubber bands or other materials snapping when over-stretched. Nylon fishing line, guitar strings, etc., may also break, flick back and cause a deep cut. For activities where there is such a risk, eye protection should be worn. It is often possible to re-design the activity to avoid the need for eye protection.

Where the children have designed and made a large construction to support, carry or contain a child (e.g. a buggy, bird-watching hide or climbing frame), it is important that the tests do not put a child at risk.

When testing or using heavy objects, place a cardboard box underneath to keep feet away. Put soft or waste material, such as bean bags or crumpled newspaper, in the box to cushion the fall.

A high fixing is often needed to work on pulley systems. Ensure that it is secure enough for the intended load.

SAFETY CODE for testing things

- Keep stretched materials away from eyes.
- Try to design activities so that eye protection is not needed. Use eye protection when this is not possible.
- When using pulleys or other hanging devices, ensure that they are attached to a secure fixing. Limit the size and load of any pulley system.
- Place a box containing soft or waste material under any hanging load. The load should itself be as low as possible, as should swinging weights (e.g. a pendulum).
- Check large constructions designed to support, carry or contain a child for strength and stability before use.
- Safely dispose of structures that have been tested to destruction or failure.
- When testing model sailing boats, do not use hand-held mains-powered fans or hairdriers. Ensure that any static mains-powered fans cannot come into contact with water.

A swinging object, such as a pendulum, can be a hazard, especially if it is heavy. Allow adequate safe space for its movement.

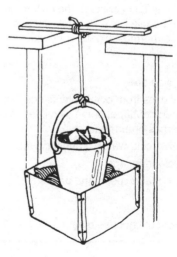

Flying things

Some flying things can be used indoors, such as paper aeroplanes and small hot-air balloons, whilst others require a large open space outdoors. Most activities with flying things require close supervision.

Do not be tempted to fly/launch out of doors under unsafe conditions, such as if it is so windy that control will be difficult or impossible. Do not put yourself or children at risk during launching/dropping.

Captive balloons and kites must not be flown above 60 metres.

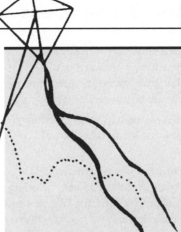

SAFETY CODE for flying things

- Teach children to aim away from each other when launching flying objects. Be aware of the added danger of children leaning out of upstairs windows and over stairwells.
- When releasing objects from a height, be sure that the children do not put themselves or others (below them) at risk. For example, they should stand on PE equipment or playground equipment rather than classroom furniture. Objects released from a height are liable to bounce – children should be warned not to lean forward.
- Spinning discs (e.g. Frisbees) and boomerangs should always be directed away from spectators, but keep in mind that they might return.

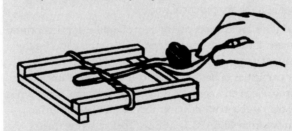

- Test catapults, ballistas and mangonels with care; use projectiles that are safe, and direct them away from spectators.

- Hot-air balloons should be filled using a hairdryer (but not a hot-air paint stripper). They can be flown indoors. Never use hot-air balloons with burning fuel.

- Never fly kites, aeroplanes and gliders near overhead power lines or electricity substations; buildings and roads may also present hazards. Other rules apply near airports.
- Do not launch rockets in windy conditions.
- Water rockets may be bought or home-made. Plastic bottles that have held carbonated drinks are more likely to withstand the pressure and less likely to split when used in home-made versions. Make sure they are directed well away from spectators when launched, to avoid panic when they come down.
- Chemically powered rockets and kits with motors for making model rockets (but not fireworks) may be safely used if you have followed the manufacturers' instructions. Never modify these motors or attempt to make such a rocket motor. Keep the rocket motors in a secure place until just before launch time in order to prevent unauthorised launches.

Batteries

Strictly speaking, a battery is several electrical cells connected together, but here we use the word in its everyday sense to include a single cell.

Obtain batteries from reputable suppliers. It is inadvisable to mix different brands and types of battery in equipment, or to use new batteries with used ones. When changing batteries in equipment, replace them all at the same time and check carefully that they are inserted the right way around. Battery technology is continually changing and you should be careful before buying novel types for use by children. Some battery types are less tolerant of misuse than others, and may explode under extreme misuse. Members can ask for advice from CLEAPSS or SSERC for types not mentioned here.

Batteries come in standard sizes such as AAA, AA, C and D (there are other equivalent codes). Batteries should not be cut open because the contents are hazardous. It is not possible to get an electric shock from a 1.5 volt battery unless a great number of them are connected together.

Coin/button batteries are a choking hazard and are unsuitable for use by young children unless securely inside equipment, e.g. in stopwatches. They might be used by older children under supervision.

Non-rechargeable (disposable) batteries are designed to be used once and then disposed of when flat. The common types are alkaline, zinc-carbon, zinc-chloride and lithium.

Lithium batteries, and *larger alkaline sizes* (sizes C and D) are not recommended for constructing classroom circuits because sustained short circuits will cause them to become hot, possibly venting violently.

Smaller alkaline batteries (sizes AAA and AA) are less likely to cause a problem if short-circuited, but they can still become hot by sustained short circuits. Alkaline batteries have a longer shelf life than zinc-chloride and zinc-carbon batteries.

Zinc-chloride and *zinc-carbon batteries* are the least likely to cause a problem if short-circuited, but they do have a shorter shelf life of roughly 18 months.

Old disposable batteries can leak corrosive materials, particularly zinc-chloride and zinc-carbon types. Consider removing the batteries from equipment such as torches and toys if they are to be unused for some time.

Rechargeable batteries have the advantage of reducing costs and waste. Batteries that are rechargeable will be labelled as such.

Nickel-metal hydride (NiMH) and *nickel-cadmium (NiCd)* types are common and come in standard sizes, including AAA and AA. However, if short-circuited, the batteries and connecting wires can become hot enough to cause burns, and a sustained short circuit will cause them to become very hot, possibly venting violently. Consequently, they are not recommended for classroom circuit work. There is no such problem when the batteries are securely inside equipment such as cameras and dataloggers, but ensure that battery compartment covers are tamper-resistant. Rechargeable batteries tend to self-discharge even if they are not used, becoming flat over time. There are low self-discharge NiMH battery types available.

There are other specialist types of rechargeable battery, e.g. lithium-ion batteries as used in laptop computers. These can be dangerous if misused and should only be used in the equipment for which they were designed. Similarly, lead-acid batteries, including car batteries, are not suitable for practical work.

Adults should supervise battery charging. It is important to use the correct charger and to place the batteries the correct way around in it. Do not put different brands or capacities of battery in the charger at the same time. Specialised chargers are available to recharge some types of disposable batteries; members should seek further advice from CLEAPSS or SSERC before trying this.

Renewable electrical energy

Small solar cells, wind turbines and wind-up generators for torches and radios, etc., are useful teaching aids and present minimal hazard.

Short circuits

Short circuits are inevitable when children are trying out circuits so it is important to choose batteries that can tolerate short circuits safely. Use just one or maybe two batteries in a circuit to limit the short-circuit current. Zinc-carbon and zinc-chloride batteries are generally the best choice to start this type of activity. The smaller size AAA and AA alkaline batteries can be used with supervision when children have become more proficient at connecting circuits; larger size alkaline, lithium, NiMH and NiCd batteries are not recommended for classroom circuit work.

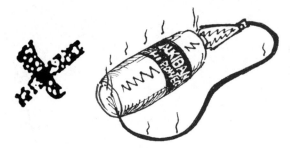

Short circuits – where battery terminals are accidentally wired together without a bulb, buzzer, motor, etc. – may cause high-power batteries to overheat

Disposal of used batteries and electrical or electronic equipment

- Batteries contain toxic materials and should be disposed of in an environmentally friendly way and not put in ordinary waste. Any shop selling more than 32 kg of batteries per year must now provide free recycling facilities without any requirement to buy new batteries.

- To reduce the amount of hazardous waste sent to landfill, electrical and electronic equipment should no longer be put in the normal refuse. It should either be taken to a recycling centre or be collected by the supplier of the replacement equipment. The supplier may charge for this.

Mains electricity

Domestic appliances may not be sufficiently robust, physically or electrically, for use in schools. All mains electrical equipment used in the classroom:

■ should be bought from a reputable source such as a recognised school supplier;

■ must be subject to a regular electrical safety test ('PAT testing') organised by the employer, which must include any appliances brought in from home; and

■ should be checked for obvious damage by the teacher or other responsible adult each time it is used.

Teach children how to handle some mains equipment. There may be instances when they will need to use such equipment regularly with very little supervision. Therefore, they need to be taught how to do this safely.

Low-voltage power supplies (e.g. 0–12 volt power packs)

Low-voltage power supplies are expensive but may be more cost-effective than using many disposable batteries if a lot of time is spent teaching electricity

Some equipment which is designed to run at low voltage may require a specific power supply, which is often included. Always follow the manufacturers' instructions.

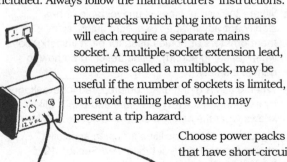

Power packs which plug into the mains will each require a separate mains socket. A multiple-socket extension lead, sometimes called a multiblock, may be useful if the number of sockets is limited, but avoid trailing leads which may present a trip hazard.

Choose power packs that have short-circuit protection and limit the current to no more than three amperes (3 amps, 3 A).

SAFETY CODE for using electricity

■ Teach children never to handle mains equipment when their hands are wet. The risk of electric shock is much greater, as the current can travel more easily through damp skin.

■ Teach children never to misuse mains electricity and warn them of electrical dangers in the home, in school and outdoors, especially in substations and from overhead cables or railway lines.

■ Teach children never to use mains equipment with a damaged plug or frayed lead. Such equipment is the most common source of accidents with electricity.

■ Teach children always to switch off both the appliance and the socket before plugging in or unplugging. Initially they should learn to do this under close adult supervision. Teach them also not to touch the pins of the plug when plugging in.

■ Mains cables should never be joined or repaired with sticky tape of any sort, but should be replaced to a professional standard. If using plug and socket extensions, be aware of trailing cables getting damaged or causing accidents through tripping, etc. A floor cable protector reduces the risk of tripping over cables.

■ Mains filament lamps (bulbs) may get hot enough to burn skin and char paper. If a hot mains lamp is splashed with water it may explode. Low-energy lamps get much less hot.

■ Teach children always to report damage and breakages.

■ Teach children who are capable how to use wire strippers and screwdrivers safely.

■ Beware of children connecting a large number of batteries together in a circuit.

■ Store batteries in such a way that their terminals cannot touch and short circuit.

■ Do not allow children to cut open batteries; their contents may be corrosive and toxic.

■ Discourage children from checking batteries by touching both terminals with their tongue.

■ Dispose of flat batteries because they may start to leak. Use a simple battery tester to identify flat batteries. Check appliances regularly for leaking batteries; the corrosive liquid will ruin equipment and may damage skin.

■ Batteries should be removed from equipment which is not in regular use.

■ Check that circuits are disconnected as soon as they are finished with.

■ Teach children how to deal with broken lamps (bulbs) (see *Dealing with broken glass* in Section 15, *Glass and alternatives*).

In the event of anyone receiving an electric shock, it is essential to switch the power off at the wall socket, before an attempt is made to help the victim. Otherwise, the rescuer may also receive an electric shock.

Aquaria

If mains-powered accessories for aquaria are used, additional safety precautions such as a residual current device (RCD) should be considered. Schools which are members can seek further advice from CLEAPSS or SSERC (see Section 20, *Bibliography* and *Further advice*).

Electrical equipment used outdoors

Electrical equipment used outdoors, such as dataloggers, should be battery powered, not mains powered. In science and technology, it should not be necessary to use mains-powered equipment outdoors.

Children need to learn how to handle glass safely. Science lessons offer an ideal opportunity for this to take place in a supervised environment. Children should not normally use glass containers for investigations but it may be appropriate on some occasions, and for these you will need a risk assessment which considers, for example, the maturity of the children and the degree of supervision available. Totally transparent containers are sometimes needed and most plastic containers are translucent.

Using glass and its alternatives safely

Normal glass containers will shatter if, for example, hot water is poured into them; they should not be used for heating substances or for transporting hot liquids. Use glassware such as ovenware or laboratory glassware (borosilicate glass such as Pyrex) which can resist such changes in temperature, or ceramic or metal containers instead.

Note that thin-walled plastic containers such as yoghurt pots may soften or even collapse if used with hot water or in microwave ovens. Lightweight containers may fall over too easily, especially if tall.

Plastic mirrors are safer than glass ones. If glass mirrors or pieces of plane glass are used at all, bind the edges and cover their backs with strong adhesive tape.

SAFETY CODE for handling glass

Dealing with broken glass

- Train children how to deal with broken glass. Teachers should consider carefully whether or not children are sufficiently mature to be allowed to clear up broken glass under close supervision.
- Ensure that a dustpan and brush are readily available when glass is in use.
- Never put unwrapped broken glass in any bin. Carefully dispose of all chipped or broken glassware. Wrap broken glass in thick layers of newspaper or seal it in a plastic tub or cardboard box and place this directly in the refuse.

Dealing with cuts and grazes

- Follow your employer's procedure for dealing with cuts and grazes.
- It is advisable to wear protective gloves when you might come into contact with blood.
- Not all cuts and grazes are cause for great concern but serious (or doubtful) cases should be dealt with by a trained first-aider.

Using glass

Teach children that glass is fragile and that broken glass may lead to cuts, possibly in turn leading to infection. If glass containers break, there may be spills of hazardous materials. Suitable control measures in the primary classroom may include the following.

- Avoid all use of glass by younger or less-reliable pupils.
- Avoid glass where satisfactory safer alternatives exist (e.g. plastic mirrors, plastic test tubes).
- For many activities, yoghurt pots, clear plastic tumblers and similar containers are cheaper and more suitable for children to use than expensive and fragile glassware.
- When going outside to collect materials, use plastic containers and never glass bottles or jars.
- Where the use of glass is unavoidable or has significant advantages (e.g. light bulbs, spirit thermometers or bottles used for pitch investigations when teaching sound), teach the children how to handle it safely.
- When glass is being used, be prepared for breakages by ensuring that everyone (staff and pupils alike) knows what they should or should not do.
- If your school has facilities for using specialist glassware such as test tubes, see Section 19, *Taking it further*.

Suitable sources of heat

Hot water from a tap, kettle or immersion heater

Hot water is probably the best heat source for use in primary schools. The water seldom needs to be anywhere near boiling, so water from the hot tap will usually be adequate. If very hot water is needed, an adult should carry it in a closed container such as a kettle or Thermos flask.

A hot-water bottle filled with warm water may be a convenient heat source for some purpose (e.g. melting chocolate or comparing insulation properties of various jacket materials) but may be damaged by very hot water and is difficult to pour from.

Hairdriers

Hairdriers are useful for filling hot-air balloons and for drying materials. They must not be used where water might enter the drier. See also Section 14, *Teaching about electricity and using electrical equipment*.

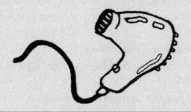

Microwave ovens, stoves such as the 'Baby Belling', electric boiling rings and popcorn makers

Each of these is useful for exploring the science in cooking, candle-making and other investigations. Suitably trained children can use microwave ovens for routine activities such as softening Play-doh. The level of supervision needed will depend on the maturity and experience of the child. See also Section 14, *Teaching about electricity and using electrical equipment*.

Tea lights and candles

Tea lights (night lights) provide a small flame or simple heat source and are much less easily knocked over than candles. During use they should stand on a layer of sand inside a large container (e.g. a metal baking tray). If candles are used, they need to be supported in a stable holder.

 ## Some sources of heat NOT recommended

Spirit burners and oil lamps

Spirit burners should not be used. Methylated spirit (industrial denatured alcohol, IDA) is highly flammable and some burners have unsafe designs.

Methylated spirit burners should not be used in model steam engines. Solid fuel is a safer alternative but do not attempt to extinguish burning tablets by blowing them out. Warn children not to handle or touch these tablets directly.

Spirit burners at home

Consider warning children of the dangers of using spirit burners in home chemistry sets or steam engines.

Picnic stoves

Types of stoves intended for outdoor use should not be used indoors.

Portable bottled-gas burners

Portable bottled-gas burners should not be used in primary schools because they are unstable and difficult to use safely.

Hot-air paint strippers

Hot-air paint strippers are very dangerous and are too powerful for use in schools.

- See the following pages for more information on heating things and the *Safety code*.
- Choose the appropriate source of heat for the activity so as to minimise the risk.
- Almost all heating activities require close adult supervision, depending on the age, maturity and experience of the children and the type of heat source being used.
- Take special care when using open (naked) flames – hair and some clothing can ignite easily.

- Heating investigations in primary science do not normally require specialist facilities and apparatus but, if using Bunsen burners in laboratory-type facilities, see Section 19, *Taking it further*.
- If you need to use a pressure cooker, e.g. for sterilising owl pellets, see Section 19, *Taking it further*.

Techniques for heating

- Hot water is a good source of heat.
- Particular care needs to be taken when heating liquids in test tubes.
- Never heat a closed container such as a corked test tube.
- Only small samples should be heated or burnt. As well as increasing the risk of accidents, it is often difficult to observe small changes when large samples are used.
- Where large quantities need to be heated and used, e.g. in candle-making, the risk is much greater and hence closer supervision is needed, depending on the age, maturity and experience of the children.
- Avoid inhaling fumes when heating substances.
- Some materials (e.g. salt) can spit, especially if heated strongly.

- If heating liquids in test tubes, beware of the risk of the contents being unexpectedly and suddenly ejected violently ('bumping').
- If you are using Bunsen burners, you will need safety spectacles or other eye protection, fire extinguishers and/or a fire blanket.
- If you are using mercury-in-glass thermometers in laboratory-type facilities, you will need access to a mercury spill kit.

For more details about all of these, see Section 19, *Taking it further*.

Using open flames

Many heating and burning activities can be successfully carried out with tea lights (night lights).

- Beware that even tea lights can ignite clothing and hair.
- Do not carry lit candles or tea lights around.
- Only adults should light candles or other sources of naked flames.
- Heating and burning activities should take place over a sand tray kept for this purpose. This will contain drips and spills and allow fires to be extinguished rapidly.
- Always ensure that there is adequate ventilation.
- Substances can be heated in metal spoons, small containers made of aluminium foil or in metal lids. If metal bottle tops are used, any lining needs to be removed and paint or varnish burnt off beforehand (e.g. by an adult roasting it out of doors). Never use more than about half a teaspoonful of the substance.

- Use a wooden clothes peg fixed to the end of a handle (made of square-section timber) to hold materials over a tea light flame.

Heating liquids in test tubes

- Whenever possible, heat the liquid by putting the test tube in a container of hot water rather than over an open flame.

- Do not fill the tube more than one-fifth full.
- Only heat test tubes of liquids over open (naked) flames if eye protection is being worn by all those nearby. Safety goggles, safety spectacles or face shields are all suitable (see Section 19, *Taking it further*).

Measuring temperature

Convenient methods of measuring temperature include:

- spirit-filled thermometers;
- liquid-crystal strips (e.g. forehead thermometers);
- thermochromic materials (e.g. mugs which change colour);
- dial types (e.g. Thermostik);
- digital thermometers, which are robust and easy to read; and
- dataloggers with temperature sensors.

Heating a thermometer above its designed temperature range, for instance by putting it in a flame, will damage it and may cause it to explode.

Breakages of liquid-in-glass thermometers can be avoided by fitting anti-roll devices, e.g. a flag made of pvc tape, at the end.

It is recommended not to use mercury-in-glass thermometers in primary science.

SAFETY CODE for heating things

- Ensure that heating activities involving naked flames or very hot water take place under close adult supervision.
- Warn children about the dangers of fire, hot apparatus, steam and hot liquids, including hot water from a tap. Check the temperature of the hot water supply. When showing steam condensing on to cold surfaces, take care not to burn yourself – use oven gloves. Warn children that boiling rings, hotplates and ceramic hobs and objects that have been heated (e.g. in a microwave oven) can burn even though they may not appear to be hot.
- If there is no running water in the classroom, it is a good idea to have a bucket of cold water available to cool burns.

- Teach children
  - what to do if they get burnt;
  - to stand when things are being heated either by themselves or during a demonstration; this will allow them to step back quickly in the event of an accident;
  - to hold objects that are being heated well away from themselves, preferably at arm's length; and
  - not to lean over a heat source in case the substance 'spits' or the substance being tested catches fire.

- Children are unlikely to need to wear eye protection when using gentle heat sources such as hot water or tea lights (night lights) but might need to do so if the material is likely to 'spit'. Teachers will need to try this in advance. For more information, see Section 19, *Taking it further*.
- Tie back long hair and avoid loose garments. Clothing may be flammable.
- Stand tea lights (or candles, if used) in a sand tray during use to promote stability and also to catch any burning fragments which may be produced when materials are burnt in a flame.
- Never leave naked flames unattended.
- Before disposing of matches, check that they are extinguished.
- When testing materials by heating, only use a small sample and have adequate ventilation because plastics, fibres and fabrics may give off hazardous fumes when burning. Teachers should test small samples in advance to ensure that it is safe for children to heat them.
- Never heat glass objects, except those made for the purpose such as Pyrex.
- If it is ever necessary to carry very hot water around the work area, only do so using a closed container such as a kettle or Thermos flask.
- Turn saucepan handles away from the front of a stove to avoid accidental spillage and fit safety rails to the stove if possible.
- Place boiling rings and stoves where they cannot be knocked, but at a suitable working height for children.
- Switch off stoves and boiling rings immediately after use.

Dealing with burns and scalds

- Act very quickly.
- Flood the affected area with cold water for at least 10 minutes or until the pain is relieved.
- Depending on the severity of the injury, you may need to summon the first-aider, who may send the casualty to hospital for urgent treatment.

Fire safety

- Pouring dry sand on to a minor fire will usually restrict or extinguish it. Fill a large plastic water or soft drink bottle with dry sand and label it
  'DRY SAND FOR EXTINGUISHING SMALL FIRES'.
- For burning hair or clothing, 'stop, drop and roll': stop the casualty running around, drop the casualty to the floor, and smother the fire with a fire blanket or similar.
- Make sure that you know the school's plans for emergencies, and that children understand the building evacuation procedure in the event of fire.

Chemical changes take place all around us, especially in the kitchen. They are both useful and fascinating. Children can learn much about the composition of materials and about classification by using 'chemicals'. This can be done safely but a risk assessment will be needed, depending on the maturity of the pupils and the supervision available (see Section 2, *Risk assessment*).

Just because a substance can be bought easily in a shop does not mean that it is safe for use in the classroom. Warn children that many household chemicals are very hazardous.

School suppliers are increasingly producing kits for making interesting materials, e.g. instant snow powder. Teachers need to check the instructions and any hazard warnings provided with such kits; if unsure, members can contact CLEAPSS or SSERC for advice (see Section 20, *Further Advice*).

Compounds used to grow crystals can be recycled.

Indicators to show acidity or alkalinity can be prepared by crushing (or, if necessary, boiling) red cabbage, beetroot, red rose petals, blackberries and many other plant materials in water and then filtering or sieving. The coloured solution is then ready for use and can be kept for a few days in a fridge. Herbal teas containing hibiscus and the juice from some canned strongly coloured fruits can also be used.

If food testing is a part of the curriculum then the following can be used safely.

- To test for vitamin C, use dcpip (a blue dye which goes colourless).
- Test for fats or oils by their ability to make paper translucent.
- Test for starch using iodine solution (iodine in a solution of potassium iodide in water, not an alcoholic tincture of iodine).

 Suitable chemicals

The following chemicals are low hazard and can be used safely by children (but remember that any substance, even salt, can be harmful if taken in sufficient quantity).

aluminium foil
baking powder (bicarbonate of soda and tartaric acid)
bath salts and bath 'bombs'
bicarbonate of soda (sodium hydrogencarbonate)
blackboard chalk (calcium sulfate or carbonate)
brass (a mixture [alloy] of copper and zinc)
carbonated (fizzy) drinks
chalk (calcium carbonate)
charcoal
clay (moist, to control dust)
copper foil or powder
cream of tartar (tartaric acid and potassium hydrogentartrate)
dcpip
Epsom salts (magnesium sulfate)
fertilisers (some of them, such as liquid household plant foods, Baby Bio)
food colouring
gelatine
glycerine (glycerol)
health salts (e.g. Andrews Liver Salts)
iron filings (avoid eye and skin contact)
lemon juice (contains citric acid)
litmus paper or solution
marble chips (calcium carbonate)

milk
oils, vegetable and mineral (but not engine oil)
Polyfilla (cellulose filler)
salt (sodium chloride)
sand
soap
steel wool
sugar
tea (contains tannic acid)
universal indicator paper
Vaseline (petroleum jelly)
vinegar (contains acetic acid, also called ethanoic acid)
vitamin C (ascorbic acid)
washing powder, flakes and liquids (hand-washing types)
washing-up liquids
wax
zinc foil

- Check the hazard warning label on bottles or packets of chemicals.
- Warn children not to put substances into their mouths, unless known to be of food quality and clean.
- Warn children to wash their hands after handling chemicals.

- Children should avoid inhaling dusts and powders as this may harm their health.
- The chemicals shown here and on the next page are not a comprehensive list of safe or unsafe substances. Teachers in member schools who want to use other chemicals can consult CLEAPSS or SSERC (see Section 20, *Further advice*). See also Section 19, *Taking it further*.

Handle with care!

- Most of the following chemicals are hazardous but may be handled with care.
- Check the label on the bottle and the safety information supplied with the chemicals.
- The teacher needs to judge whether sufficiently close adult supervision can be exercised, given the age, maturity and experience of the class.
- Secure storage is essential to prevent unauthorised use.
- Avoid eye and skin contact as most are irritant.

For growing crystals

copper sulfate [HARMFUL]
ferrous sulfate (iron(II) sulfate) [HARMFUL]
manganese sulfate [HARMFUL]
potash alum (aluminium potassium sulfate)
Rochelle salt (potassium sodium tartrate)
sodium thiosulfate [gives TOXIC gas with acids]
zinc sulfate [HARMFUL]

Flammable liquids

The following are flammable. Under no circumstances should they be put near a naked flame. Store with care out of sunlight and away from direct heat.

iodine tincture (in alcohol)
metal polish [IRRITANT]
methylated spirit (industrial denatured alcohol, IDA; also known as ethanol)
nail varnish remover (acetone/propanone)
paraffin
some paints and varnishes
spray adhesives
surgical spirit
universal indicator solution
white spirit (turpentine substitute, 'turps')

Other materials

Alka-Seltzer [contains aspirin]
citric acid crystals [IRRITANT]
cobalt chloride paper [TOXIC]
cement [IRRITANT] and concrete
cold-water dyes [will stain skin and clothing]
iodine solution (in water) [will stain skin and clothing]
lead shot or lead foil [TOXIC]
Milton (hypochlorite solution)
plaster of Paris [there are no problems with small-scale use in investigations, but for modelling see Section 12, *Making things*]
slaked lime (garden lime) [IRRITANT]
sodium silicate (water glass) [CORROSIVE if undiluted]
washing soda (sodium carbonate) [IRRITANT]

Kits

kits for making interesting chemicals [hazards vary – members can check with CLEAPSS or SSERC if unsure of suitability for different age groups; see Section 20, *Further advice*]

 Dangerous chemicals

These household chemicals can be especially hazardous, although formulations may vary. Consider warning the children about the dangers in their homes. Draw attention to the hazard warning symbols. The hazard will depend on the exact formulation. For many of them, eye protection and (disposable, preferably nitrile) gloves would be required. In the classroom, they should only be used by the teacher, if at all. Use safer alternatives, where possible.

bleach (and cleaners containing bleach) [IRRITANT]
caustic soda (sodium hydroxide) [CORROSIVE]
de-rusting solutions [check the label]
dishwasher powders, gels and tablets [IRRITANT]
disinfectants (most general, household) [IRRITANT]
dry-cleaning fluids [check the label]
fertilisers (some) (see the *Safety code for gardening* in Section 6, *Studies out of the classroom*)
fireworks, sparklers and some party poppers [EXPLOSIVE]
hydrogen peroxide [IRRITANT]
oven cleaners (contain caustic soda) [CORROSIVE]
paint strippers [check the label]
pesticides, fungicides and insecticides [check the label]
scale removers (except those containing citric acid) [check the label]
some plant growth substances, e.g. rooting powders [check the label]
toilet cleaners [CORROSIVE]
wallpaper paste [usually contains fungicides]
weedkillers [HARMFUL]
washing powders and gels (biological or automatic)

 ## Dealing with chemicals in or on the body

- Act quickly.
- For chemicals in the eye, wash with running water from a tap for at least 10 minutes. Call the first-aider.

- For chemicals in the mouth, perhaps swallowed, only rinse the casualty's mouth with water (do not make the casualty vomit). Call the first-aider.
- For chemicals on the skin, wash thoroughly. Call the first-aider if the skin appears to be burnt.

SAFETY CODE for handling chemicals

Using chemicals

- Take care not to contaminate one chemical with another, e.g. by using an unwashed spoon.
- Dispense small quantities of chemicals. Never return excess chemical to its container.
- Transfer solid chemicals using small spoons, such as plastic teaspoons, kept for this purpose (never use your fingers). Usually, about a quarter of a teaspoon will be enough.
- Pour liquids carefully. Avoid using droppers because of the risk of careless use or deliberate misuse.
- Prevent contact with the eyes; this can happen when fingers are contaminated with chemicals.
- Wear eye protection if chemicals are likely to spit out of a tube, e.g. when heating crystals.
- Avoid skin contact and use protective gloves if the information on the substance indicates that it is corrosive or irritating to skin or is poisonous by skin absorption.
- Wipe up any spillage at once.
- Wash hands after using chemicals.
- It may be dangerous to mix chemicals. Even inadvertent mixing in a sink, etc., of household chemicals such as bleach with other cleaners or acid can produce chlorine, a toxic gas. Teachers wishing to mix chemicals should seek advice from CLEAPSS or SSERC (see Section 20, *Further advice*). Warn children of the dangers.
- Do not accept unsolicited gifts of chemicals.

Storing chemicals

- Always store hazardous chemicals in containers securely labelled with the name of the chemical, and the relevant hazard warning symbol if appropriate (see illustration). It is best to use the original container.
- Be aware of the risk of confusion and avoid using new or recycled food or drink containers for the storage of hazardous chemicals.
- Foodstuffs intended for science investigations should be so labelled and not eaten.
- Keep only small quantities of hazardous chemicals and maintain a record of them.
- Store all hazardous chemicals in a locked cupboard or room, away from heat sources, and separate from those intended as foodstuffs.
- If it is necessary to stock more than half a litre of a highly flammable liquid, it must be locked in a flame-resistant store or cupboard.

Hazard warning symbols

 Corrosive

 Harmful/irritant

 Toxic

 Highly flammable

 Explosive

 Dangerous for the environment

- Teach children to recognise the international hazard warning symbols, which they may come across on containers of hazardous chemicals (but note that not all containers of hazardous chemicals will be labelled).
- The square symbols are gradually changing over the next few years to the diamond symbols but the hazards of some chemicals will be reclassified at the same time.
- Reading the labels on containers or in catalogues and following their advice will usually provide sufficient information to control the risks as required by regulations.

Disposing of chemicals

- Small amounts of household chemicals that dissolve in water can be flushed down the drain.
- Disposal of hazardous chemicals, including liquids that don't mix with water, is controlled by law to avoid polluting the environment.

- If you have chemicals you wish to dispose of, consult either a local authority adviser or, if a member, CLEAPSS or SSERC (see Section 20, *Further advice*).

What the law requires

The Health and Safety at Work Act and its various regulations apply in primary schools as much as in any other workplace. The legislation requires employers to protect their employees, that is teachers, teaching assistants, caretakers, etc., and to extend the same protection to others who may be affected, such as parents helping in the classroom and, of course, the children.

Teachers and other employees must cooperate with their employer on health and safety matters. This means that if your employer disagrees with the advice in this book, you must follow your employer's requirements, although you are perfectly entitled to argue your case and, in doing so, members can call on the support of ASE, CLEAPSS or SSERC (see Section 20, *Further advice*) as appropriate.

For example, some education employers have suggested that glass should never be used in primary schools. Glass containers may well be inappropriate in some contexts but a risk assessment that looks at the context is more sensible than a ban. However, any such blanket ban by the employer must be respected. If you think it is unnecessarily restrictive, consult ASE, CLEAPSS or SSERC.

In all school situations there is an overriding duty of care which means that teachers and other employees must take reasonable care to ensure their own health and safety and that of others, especially the children.

For example, a teacher who departs from an agreed scheme of work without any discussion and asks the children to use poisonous seeds to investigate plant growth, rather than the specified peas or beans, is likely to be in breach of the duty of care.

Teachers must be careful for their own safety and that of others, such as caretakers, when moving heavy or awkwardly shaped items, mounting displays at high levels, etc.

Employees also have a duty to inform their employers (usually via their headteacher or curriculum coordinator)

of any defects in equipment or in systems of work, e.g. cracked electrical sockets or uneven floors. Equally, a scheme of work that fails to give advice on seeds suitable for classroom use should be reported.

Employers expecting their schools to use the latest edition of *Be safe!* will be giving appropriate advice.

Health and safety policies

Employers must have a health and safety policy. Local authorities responsible for education will have a global policy within which individual schools should have their own policy. School health and safety policies (whether or not a school is within an education/local authority) will need to refer to science and technology. This may be as part of a whole-school policy, as a separate document or as part of a science/technology policy. Although much may be covered in a general policy, science health and safety policies are likely to:

■ outline the approach to risk assessment and control measures, including how the significant findings of risk assessment are to be recorded;

■ identify any particular hazards;

■ indicate how new staff are to be inducted and other staff trained; and

■ specify how implementation is to be monitored and by whom.

It is not, for example, sufficient just to have a copy of the latest edition of *Be safe!* on the shelves. Ideally, each teacher might have her or his own copy but in any case it must be read and its advice **incorporated into schemes of work and lesson plans**. Headteachers or other managers need to check that the advice is then put into practice. From time to time, the policy needs to be reviewed for its effectiveness. This will usually involve whole-staff discussion.

Schools will find the *Be safe! INSET Pack*, published by the ASE, valuable in raising awareness amongst staff (see Section 20, *Bibliography*).

Accidents and emergencies

All members of staff need to know what to do in the unlikely event of an accident or an emergency. This should appear in the health and safety policy and it is likely that employers will have issued guidance on this. Most teachers are not trained first-aiders, with up-to-date certificates, as defined in the regulations. They are therefore not qualified to administer first aid. However, whilst waiting for a first-aider to arrive, teachers and others must be prepared to take action in emergencies, as a part of their duty of care. This is sometimes called immediate remedial measures. Where relevant, this book gives appropriate guidance.

Enhancing the curriculum

■ Science clubs, science weeks and visiting scientists can sometimes encourage work outside the normal curriculum. This can also arise when collaborating with neighbouring secondary schools or if a school has access to unusually specialist accommodation.

■ All of these can result in hazards and risks not generally encountered in primary school science and technology and not covered in the risk assessments in the main sections of this book.

■ For more information, see Section 19, *Taking it further*. Members can also consult CLEAPSS or (in Scotland) SSERC.

Primary/secondary liaison

Increasingly, primary school classes visit a neighbouring secondary school for taster lessons or a teacher from the secondary school visits a feeder primary school, often bringing in equipment and materials that would not otherwise be available. Secondary teachers need to have realistic expectations of what can be achieved in the time available, given the background and experience of the children. They need to ensure that children are likely to have the necessary knowledge and understanding to learn from an activity, not just to experience or be entertained by it.

Primary pupils and their teachers visiting secondary schools

Visits by primary pupils and their teachers to secondary schools need to be carefully discussed by all the teachers involved from both schools. A suitable risk assessment, going beyond what is normal in secondary schools must be agreed, taking account of the lack of prior laboratory (or workshop) experience, the physical size of the children and what can be realistically achieved in the limited time available. It is counterproductive to attempt to include many of the activities that pupils find enjoyable in the early years of secondary school. Teachers and teaching assistants accompanying children can help them by studying the whole of this section before the visit. Bear in mind:

- eye protection is likely to be needed but may not be a good fit on smaller faces;
- time will be needed to induct children into appropriate laboratory or workshop behaviour and teach them the safety rules;
- secondary teachers will not know which of the children present behavioural problems or may not understand instructions;
- children will not know how to use Bunsen burners safely and some will be very excited – and others fearful – at their first use of Bunsen burners; they will need time-consuming training in techniques such as heating test tubes safely; and
- visiting children may not be able to reach working surfaces comfortably.

Secondary teachers working in primary schools

When secondary teachers are working in primary schools, all the teachers involved from both schools need to discuss carefully how the planned activities will support the teaching in the primary school.

A risk assessment will need to be agreed, especially where activities go beyond the scope of *Be safe!* It may need to take account of the fact that primary classrooms:

- may not have running water, e.g. for cooling burns;
- may not have facilities for rinsing eyes;
- will almost certainly not have heating facilities except hot water or tea lights (night lights) in trays of sand;
- may lack good ventilation;
- may not have suitable fire extinguishers or fire blankets;
- may have the walls (or ceiling) covered with (flammable) displays;
- may have carpets on the floor;
- may have smoke alarms;
- will not have chemical spill kits available;
- will probably not have safety spectacles or other eye protection (and any brought in from the secondary school may be too large on children with small heads);
- may have tables more crowded together than in most laboratories;
- may not have sufficient space for children to sit at a safe distance from demonstrations; and
- may have tables on which children eat food.

When taking equipment or chemicals from the secondary school to local primary establishments, it will be necessary to pack bottles so they cannot fall over, to use containers which would contain spills and to carry a spill kit. There are restrictions on the amounts of some chemicals which can be carried. Consult CLEAPSS or SSERC (see Section 20, *Further advice*) or the RSC publication *Transporting Chemicals for Lecture Demonstrations & Similar Purposes* (see Section 20, *Bibliography*).

Working in specialist accommodation

Some schools have facilities that are more akin to secondary school laboratories (or workshops) and which allow them to take things further than is possible in ordinary primary classrooms. This might happen, for example, in all-through schools, some middle schools and prep schools. This raises additional health and safety issues which are not fully dealt with in earlier parts of this book. This section gives a brief summary of some of the key issues but they are dealt with much more fully in *Safeguards in the School Laboratory*, also published by ASE.

Schools may need to develop a set of appropriate laboratory rules and teachers may need specific hands-on training, e.g. in the use of fire extinguishers.

Bunsen burners

Bunsen burners provide a hotter and more controllable heat source and allow a much wider range of activities but introduce many new hazards.

- Remind children about the *Safety code for heating things* in Section 6, *Heating and burning*.
- Children must stand up when using Bunsen burners (those in wheelchairs, or with other mobility issues, need added protection).
- Stand the Bunsen burner on a heat-resistant mat towards the back of the bench, where it is less likely to ignite hair and clothing.
- To light a Bunsen burner, close the air-hole, and bring the lighting flame from the side.
- For gentle heating, half open the air-hole; only use a fully open air-hole for strong heating.
- When not actually heating, close the air hole to make the flame easily visible.

Laboratory glassware

Check glassware for cracks, chips and flaws which may cause injury or make it more liable to fail.

Eye protection

- Eye protection should be worn when heating liquids or chemicals likely to 'spit' with Bunsen burners.
- Teachers must rigorously enforce this.
- Safety goggles, safety spectacles or face shields must fit small faces (most do not) and conform to BS EN 166.

Accidents

The room should have suitable facilities for:

- irrigating eyes in the event of an accident;
- flooding burnt skin with cold water; and
- washing hands after working with chemicals.

Heating test tubes

- Usually only a gentle flame is needed: half close the air-hole and reduce the gas flow.
- Protect the eyes with safety goggles, safety spectacles or a face shield.
- Hold the test tube in a proper test-tube holder of suitable size; do not use a holder made of folded paper or card.
- Do not fill the tube more than one-fifth full.
- Point the mouth of the tube away from the user and from anyone else. There is a significant risk of the contents spitting out.
- Shake the tube gently while it is in the flame. If it contains a liquid, this will ensure that the liquid is at an even temperature throughout. If this is not done, the water (usually) at the bottom of the tube nearest the flame will boil and, as it turns to steam, it may suddenly force out the rest of the contents ('bumping').
- To reduce the risk of 'bumping', it is sometimes helpful to add two or three (inert) anti-bumping granules.
- Remove the tube from the flame whenever vibrations are felt, and then return it as they die down.

Heating using tripods

- Objects placed on a tripod are easily knocked over, especially if a thermometer or stirring rod is placed in a container that stands on the tripod.
- Children must stand up when using tripods.
- Tripods remain hot for a long time after the Bunsen burner is turned off.

Fire fighting

Any room in which Bunsen burners are used will usually need to have appropriate fire-fighting equipment in the vicinity. This is likely to include at least one 2 kg carbon dioxide extinguisher and a fire blanket.

Chemicals

It is likely that schools with laboratory-type facilities will want to use a wider range of chemicals than are covered in Section 17, *Chemicals*.

- Hazardous chemicals must be stored securely, keeping incompatible chemicals apart from each other.
- Schools will need to consult, and if necessary customise, their employer's risk assessments.
- Members can consult CLEAPSS or, in Scotland, SSERC (see Section 20, *Further advice*), who can advise as appropriate.

Spill kits

- If mercury-in-glass thermometers are used, schools will need to have access to an appropriate spill kit to deal with breakages.
- Different spill kits will be needed to deal with spills of other chemicals.

Pressure cookers

Pressure cookers are useful, e.g. for sterilising owl pellets. However, it will usually be most convenient to ask for the sterilisation to be done in the science department of your local secondary school.

Taking biology further: cheek cells

Schools which want to sample pupils' cheek cells will need to consult and, if necessary, customise their employer's risk assessments. Consider how well the pupils can be trusted to follow instructions and the level of supervision necessary. The following procedure is widely used.

- Rub a cotton bud from a newly opened pack over the inside of the mouth.
- Wipe the bud on a microscope slide, stain and apply a cover slip, and place the used bud immediately into disinfectant (use Milton).
- After the cells have been observed, immerse the slide and cover slip in a beaker of disinfectant.
- After at least 15 minutes of disinfection, wearing gloves, transfer the used cotton buds into a polythene bag that is sealed and disposed of into normal refuse.
- The slides (and possibly cover slips) should be washed thoroughly, dried and reused as appropriate.

Taking biology further: microbiology

Schools should only contemplate culturing samples from the environment or fingers and equivalent body surfaces on agar plates in Petri dishes if they have access to an autoclave or pressure cooker to ensure safe preparation and disposal. Teachers would also need training in aseptic (sterile) techniques, etc. Members should consult CLEAPSS or SSERC for further advice (see Section 20, *Further advice*).

Power tools

Schools with suitable workshop-type facilities may consider allowing children to use power tools such as pillar drills, scroll saws and belt facers (sanders).

- Teachers must be trained in the safe use of all machinery.
- Children need close supervision by a trained person.
- Some machines will need local exhaust ventilation, i.e. dust extraction.
- Eye protection may well be necessary.

20 Bibliography

Note that all CLEAPSS publications are available free to members from the *Primary Resource* section of the CLEAPSS website (and on short-term loan in Scotland to members of SSERC).

SSERC publications on many of the sections below are available to members on the SSERC *SafetyNet* website, although they may not have exactly the same titles and categories.

3 Teaching health and safety

L241 *Teaching Health and Safety in Primary Schools*, 2004 (CLEAPSS)

Safer Children in a Digital World: The report of the Byron Review, 2008 (DCSF) http://www.dcsf.gov.uk/byronreview/

Use of display screen equipment by children (SSERC)

5 Ourselves and our senses

L245 *Ourselves*, 2005 (CLEAPSS)

E261 *Body Parts: Instructions and Templates for Cut and Stick Human Body Parts*, 2010 (CLEAPSS)

Materials of Living Origin. Pupils as Subjects of Experiment or Investigation (SSERC)

6 Studies out of the classroom

Avoiding Ill Health at Open Farms – Advice to Farmers (with Teachers' Supplement) (AIS 23/AIS23 Supplement) http://www.hse.gov.uk/pubns/ais23.pdf

Health and Safety of Pupils on Educational Visits, 1998 (DfEE)

Educational Visits: Best Practice 2009. Available from all the Northern Ireland Education & Library Boards: http://www.belb.org.uk/teachers/Educational_Visits.asp http://www.neelb.org.uk/schools/schoolsbranch/publications/ http://www.seelb.org.uk/board_publications/bp.htm http://www.welbni.org/index.cfm/go/publications/alpha/E http://www.selb.org/publications/documents/ EducationVisits2009.pdf

Health & Safety on Educational Excursions: a Good Practice Guide, 2004 (Scottish Executive), ISBN 0 7559 4363 5

Educational Visits: A Safety Guide for Learning Outside the Classroom. All Wales Guidance, 2010 (Welsh Assembly Government)
Ymweliadau addysgol. Arweiniad i ddiogelwch wrth ddysgu tu allan i'r ystafell ddosbarth. Canllawiau Cymru gyfan, 2010 http://wales.gov.uk/topics/educationandskills/ allsectorpolicies/healthandsafety/ educationalvisits/?lang=en ; [ibid] /?lang=cy

The Countryside Code at http://www.naturalengland.org. uk/ourwork/enjoying/default.aspx

NHS Direct gives information on areas of the country where Lyme disease is a significant risk http://www.nhs.uk/Conditions/Lyme-disease/Pages/ Introduction.aspx

Group Safety at Water Margins (DfES) http://www.teachers.gov.uk/_doc/3820/Group%20 Safety%20at%20Water%20Margins.pdf

Information and teaching resources from Cancer Research UK at http://www.sunsmart.org.uk

Safety in out-of-school science, R. Vincent and J. Wray, *School Science Review* (1988) **250**(70), 55. Available on the ASE website http://www.ase.org.uk/resources/health-and-safety-resources/health-and-safety-primary-science/

The Safe School Travel Pack and *Safe School Trips*, 1996 (Scottish School Board Association)

Materials of Living Origin. Surveying and Collecting Living Material from the Environment for Investigation (SSERC)

Farm visits: health & safety issues. J. Richardson, *Primary Science Review* (2000) **62**(March/April), 20–22

Safety and the school pond. P. Bunyan, *Primary Science Review* (1988) **7**(Summer), 21–22 (originally in *School Science Review* (1987) **247**(69), 286). Available on the ASE website http://www.ase.org.uk/resources/health-and-safety-resources/health-and-safety-primary-science/

Visits and resources for food and farming, K Hann, *Primary Science Review* (2000) **62**(March/April), 14–16

L190 *Studying Microorganisms in Primary Schools*, 1997 (CLEAPSS) gives guidance on composting

L221 *Developing and Using Environmental Areas in School Grounds*, 1998 (CLEAPSS)

PS17 *Viewing the Sun*, 2004 (CLEAPSS)
PS86a *Farm animals in Schools and on Visits* (primary), 2009 (CLEAPSS)

8 Microorganisms

L190 *Studying Microorganisms in Primary Schools*, 1997 (CLEAPSS)

Microbiological Techniques (SSERC) (provides some background, but is mainly relevant to secondary schools)

9 Plants

Poisonous Plants and Fungi: An Illustrated Guide (2nd edition), Marion R. Cooper, Anthony W. Johnson and Elizabeth A. Dauncey, 2003 (TSO), ISBN 9780117028616

L42 *Plants for Primary Science*, 2009 (CLEAPSS)

10 Keeping animals

Animals in Schools – a Teacher's Guide to the Educational and Therapeutic Benefits. The Society for Companion Animal Studies (SCAS), The Blue Cross, Shilton Road, Burford OX18 4PF

L52 *Small Mammals*, 2007 (CLEAPSS)
L71 *Incubating and Hatching Eggs*, 2006 (CLEAPSS)
L181 *Cold Water Aquaria*, 1990 (CLEAPSS)
L197 *Giant African Land Snails*, 2006 (CLEAPSS)
L201 *Giant Millipedes*, 1992 (CLEAPSS)
L206 *Tadpoles*, 2009 (CLEAPSS)
L213 *Science with Minibeasts: Snails*, 1995 (CLEAPSS)
L227 *Stick Insects*, 1992 (CLEAPSS)
L257 *Science with Minibeasts: Earthworms*, 2008 (CLEAPSS)
PS55 *Bringing Pets and Other Animals into Schools*, 2002 (CLEAPSS)
PS87 *Bees and Beekeeping in Schools*, 2009 (CLEAPSS)

The British Beekeepers' Association publications are available at http://www.britishbee.org.uk

Materials of Living Origin 2. Keeping Animals in Schools (SSERC), particularly the chapters 'Procedures for taking animals home' and 'Examples of protocols for care of animals at home'

The RSPCA produces a number of useful books on studying animals. Many can be downloaded from http://www.rspca.org.uk – search under 'Teachers'

11 Using animal materials

Materials of Living Origin – Educational Uses. A Code of Practice for Scottish Schools (SSERC)

12 Making things

Make it Safe! (5th edition), 2001. A companion volume to *Be safe!* relating to design and technology activities. Published by The National Association of Advisers and Inspectors in Design and Technology. It can be ordered from NAAIDT Publications, c/o DATA, 16 Wellesbourne House, Walton Road, Wellesbourne CV35 9JB. Tel: 01789 473912

L18   *Glues and Adhesives*, 2000 (CLEAPSS)

L111   *Tools and Techniques*, 2007 (CLEAPSS)

L247   *Make It and Use It*, 2006 (CLEAPSS)

PS74   *Plaster of Paris in Primary Schools*, 2007 (CLEAPSS)

13 Forces and motion

G161   *Magnets in Primary Schools*, 2009 (CLEAPSS)

14 Teaching about electricity and using electrical equipment

L86p   *Electrical Safety*, 1995 (CLEAPSS)

L112p   *Batteries and LV Units – Which to Buy*, 2001 (CLEAPSS)

L124   *Aquaria – Electrical Safety*, 1999 (CLEAPSS)

16 Heating and burning

L157p   *Measuring Temperature*, 2001 (CLEAPSS)

17 Chemicals

G5p   *Using Chemicals Safely*, 2010 (CLEAPSS)

PS74   *Plaster of Paris in Primary Schools*, 2007 (CLEAPSS)

PS81   *Fireworks and Explosives*, 2008 (CLEAPSS)

18 Managing health and safety

Be safe! INSET Pack (2nd edition), 2002 (ASE), ISBN 978 0 863573 38 5 (there is an update for this edition of *Be safe!* at http://www.ase.org.uk/resources/health-and-safety-resources/health-and-safety-primary-science/)

L224   *Model Health and Safety Policies for Primary Science*, 2006 (CLEAPSS)

PS22   *Health and Safety in Primary Science and Technology*, 2006 (CLEAPSS)

Emergency Aid in Schools (6th edition), 2006 (St John Ambulance)

First Aid Manual (9th edition), 2009 (Dorling Kindersley), authorised manual of St John Ambulance, St Andrew's Ambulance Association and the British Red Cross, ISBN 978 14053 35379

Guidance on First Aid for Schools, 1988 (DfEE) http://www.teachernet.gov.uk/wholeschool/healthandsafety/firstaid/

Managing Medicines in Schools and Early Years Settings, 2005 (DfES) http://www.teachernet.gov.uk/wholeschool/healthandsafety/medical/

Supporting Pupils with Medication Needs, 2008 (Department of Education, Northern Ireland) http://www.deni.gov.uk

The Administration of Medicines in Schools, 2006 (The Scottish Government) http://www.scotland.gov.uk

Access to Education and Support for Children and Young People with Medical Needs, 2010 (Welsh Assembly Government) http://www.wales.gov.uk

19 Taking it further

Safeguards in the School Laboratory (11th edition), 2006 (ASE), ISBN 978 0 86357 408 5

Transporting Chemicals for Lecture Demonstrations & Similar Purposes, 2008 (Royal Society of Chemistry) http://www.rsc.org/images/safetybooklet_tcm18-115083.pdf

Further advice

Members may obtain advice on health and safety matters from the following organisations and their regular journals, newsletters and other publications.

The Association for Science Education (ASE) *(publisher of Be safe!)*
College Lane, Hatfield AL10 9AA
Tel: 01707 283000; E-mail: info@ase.org.uk; Website: http://www.ase.org.uk
Membership is open to anyone interested in science education. Primary schools can have a group membership. The ASE publishes *Primary Science* (formerly *Primary Science Review*) and *Education in Science*, both five times a year. It also publishes many books to support the teaching of science in primary schools.

CLEAPSS (sponsor of the 4th edition of *Be safe!*)
The Gardiner Building, Brunel Science Park, Kingston Lane, Uxbridge UB8 3PQ
Tel: 01895 251496; E-mail: science@cleapss.org.uk; Website: http://www.cleapss.org.uk
Membership is open to education authorities, and hence all of their schools, throughout the UK (except Scotland). Independent schools and teacher-training establishments may join as associate members. CLEAPSS publishes *Primary Science and Technology Newsletter* termly, which is distributed free to all subscribing local authority and associate schools.

SSERC (sponsor of the 4th edition of *Be safe!*)
2 Pitreavie Court, South Pitreavie Business Park, Dunfermline KY11 8UB
Tel: 01383 626070; E-mail: sts@sserc.org.uk; Websites: http://www.sserc.org.uk, http://www.science3-18.org/
SSERC is a consortium of Scottish education authorities and provides services to elected members, officers, teachers, student teachers and technicians. Independent schools and colleges may also subscribe. SSERC publishes the *Primary Science and Technology Bulletin*, which is distrubuted free to all members..

Index

Index